THE
STUDENT
COOKBOOK

Bounty
BOOKS

The Student Cookbook

Publisher: Samantha Warrington
Managing Editor: Karen Rigden
Assistant Production Manager: Caroline Alberti
Editor: Jane Birch
Designer: Chris Bell/cbdesign

First published in 2015 by Bounty Books,
a division of Octopus Publishing Group Ltd
Carmelite House
50 Victoria Embankment
London, EC4Y 0DZ
www.octopusbooks.co.uk

Reprinted in 2016

An Hachette UK Company
www.hachette.co.uk

ISBN: 978-0-753726-15-0

Printed and bound in China

Drinking excessive alcohol can significantly
damage your health. The UK Health
Department recommends that men do not
regularly exceed 3–4 units a day and women
2–3 units. Never operate a vehicle when
you have been drinking alcohol. Octopus
Publishing Group accepts no liability or
responsibility for any consequences resulting
from the use of or reliance on the information
contained herein.

THE STUDENT COOKBOOK

contents

Introduction

There's way more to student cooking than beans, breakfast cereal and biscuits. With the help of this easy-to-follow guide you will pick up a few culinary skills, learn to experiment in the kitchen and enjoy some great home-cooking along the way.

There are over 100 recipes for everything from curries and cakes to cocktails and casseroles, but you don't always have to follow a recipe. Once you have some kitchen confidence, you can knock up a pasta dish with whatever is on hand in the freezer or use leftover veg, a can of pulses and a stock cube as the basis of a simple and filling winter-warming soup. And remember, if you have eggs, you have a meal, be it a fried egg on toast or a fluffy omelette.

kitchen equipment

You don't need to spend a fortune getting together a battery of equipment that would make a chef happy; you just need to start with the basics and buy, beg or borrow anything else you might need as you go along and your cooking repertoire gets bigger.

Chopping board Plastic is the cheapest and easiest to wash.

Knives A large, serrated one for cutting bread and cake; a medium-sized knife for chopping vegetables and cutting up meat and a small knife for chopping fruit and fiddly things like garlic and chillies.

Cutlery for eating.

Frying pan Non-stick helps when it comes to washing up and it should be large with a lid.

Small saucepan for things like porridge, sauces and scrambled egg.

Large saucepan with a lid. If you can afford it, two saucepans make life easier.

Large bowl for mixing, which can double as a salad bowl or a serving bowl.

roasting tray and, if you are going to bake, cake tins.
veg peeler, fish slice, a couple of wooden spoons, potato masher, balloon whisk, can opener and bottle opener.
for keeping food and leftovers in the fridge, a plastic lunchbox for food on the go.
for pasta bakes, stews and so on.
side plate, cereal bowl, egg cup.

There are some everyday ingredients that you'll use time and again so it is worth making sure you have them to hand.

fresh stuff

- Bacon or sausages
- Bread
- Butter or spread
- Cheese
- Eggs
- Fruit
- Veg (you will use onions, potatoes and garlic regularly)
- Yogurt

in the freezer

- Peas, sweetcorn and/or other frozen vegetables
- Fish and meat
- Bread (pitta bread and sliced bread are good standbys)

in the cupboard

- Breakfast cereal
- Cans (baked beans, tuna, chopped tomatoes, pulses, etc)
- Coffee
- Couscous
- Dried herbs (mixed herbs, oregano and thyme)
- Dried pasta and noodles
- Flour
- Hot chocolate
- Jam, honey and spreads
- Oil (olive and sunflower)
- Quinoa
- Rice
- Salt and pepper
- Sauces and condiments (ketchup, mayo, wholegrain or Dijon mustard, brown sauce, soy sauce)
- Stock cubes or powder
- Spices (cinnamon, chilli and curry powder or paste)
- Sugar
- Teabags
- Tomato purée
- Vinegar

nutrition

Being a student on a budget doesn't mean you have a reason to eat badly. If you don't eat properly, you could become over- or under-weight and poor eating habits lead to illness from a weakened immune system and to reduced mental ability, meaning you find it hard to concentrate.

You may think it's expensive to eat well, but it's actually cheaper. The supermarket is full of good-for-you products (low fat, low sugar and high fibre) that will cost you less than those sugary, fatty, processed foods packed with 'empty' calories and few nutrients.

Aim to get your 5 a day of a wide variety of fruit and vegetables. Snack on fresh fruit instead of biscuits or crisps. Bin the takeaways, except as a treat, and cook your own meals. To pad out a meal, use cans of lentils or add a portion of protein-rich quinoa or rice, pasta, couscous or potatoes. Beans, lentils and nuts are all good sources of protein and fibre, as are eggs, fish and poultry.

Overdosing on caffeine will not benefit you, so try to limit your cups of coffee to 2 or 3 a day.

hygiene matters

Use common sense and follow these simple guidelines to avoid food poisoning or the kitchen attracting flies or, even worse, rodents:

Keep it clean: make sure that the kitchen counters and floor and the fridge – all ideal breeding grounds for bacteria – are cleaned regularly and that the rubbish bin is emptied often. And don't forget about washing tea towels and cleaning cloths, as germs love these too.

Wash your hands: make sure you wash your hands before you start cooking.

Wash fruit and veg: just think about all the people who will have handled these before they get to you and make sure you wash them.

Defrost meat in the fridge, rather than leaving it out on the kitchen counter.

Pack away chilled and frozen food in the fridge or freezer as soon as you get home.

Keep raw meat covered and on the lowest shelf of the fridge, away from other food to prevent contamination.

Use airtight plastic containers or clingfilm for storing leftovers.

If something looks or smells bad, don't eat it!

crash course in cookery terms

Here's the lowdown on a few key cookery terms and techniques to give your culinary skills a boost:

Al dente: cooked just long enough so still firm to the bite.

Baste: this means brushing food with oil or marinade while it is cooking to keep it moist and add flavour.

Cream: this term is used in baking and means beating the butter or margarine with sugar with a wooden spoon (or electric mixer, if you are lucky enough to have one) until it is a pale colour and creamy smooth.

Marinate: a way of getting extra flavour into fish, meat or chicken by leaving it to soak in a sauce – for example, jerk seasoning or a mix of olive oil and lemon – before cooking.

Season: this means adding salt and pepper, though sometimes a recipe will say to season with spices. The trick is to add a little at a time and taste as you go along.

Simmer: to cook over a low heat so that bubbles break the surface.

Stir-fry: to cook thinly sliced veg and meat or fish in a little oil in a wok or large frying pan for just few minutes, stirring all the time for even cooking.

how do I know if its cooked?

Chicken, turkey and pork must be thoroughly cooked before serving. To test whether meat and poultry are cooked, insert a skewer or thin-bladed knife into the thickest part of the meat. For a whole chicken, skewer through the thickest part of the drumstick into the breast meat and then wait a few seconds – if the juices run clear, it is ready. If there are any traces of pink, then it needs a little longer. Cook for 10 minutes more, then test again. For pork chops or a joint of pork, insert the skewer into the centre, then check the meat juices in the same way.

Beef and lamb can be eaten slightly pink, according to your personal preference.

Fish is cooked through when it is the same colour all the way through and the flesh breaks easily into flakes. Uncooked prawns will turn pink all over when cooked through.

budgeting

Sticking to a budget may sound boring, but it's a necessary part of student life. Here are some pointers to bear in mind.

SAVVY SHOPPING
To help you stick to your budget, it pays to shop wisely:

Make a list and stick to it. Before leaving for the supermarket, make a list of the things you need. When you get there, make sure you only buy what's on the list and nothing else. Don't be tempted to buy items on impulse just because they catch your eye.

Costing

Cost
£

To help you budget, each recipe in this book is given a rating of £, ££ or £££. The ones marked £ are your go-to recipes for when funds are low. At the other end of the scale, £££ marks the recipes ideal for those 'I deserve a treat' occasions.

Don't buy more than you can afford or than you can eat while it is still fresh – it's a good idea to take cash with you, and only enough to cover what you need to buy so you can't spend any more.

Don't go shopping when you're hungry either, or you'll need up with unnecessary items going through the checkout!

Check out market stalls and farmers' markets as you may find cheap fruit and veg there.

Pick up supermarket bargains towards closing time when items are being discounted! Also, look out for special offers, such as buy-one-get-one-free, at the supermarket, but only buy them if they are things you will actually eat, otherwise they will be wasted.

Prep & cook times

You'll need to have some idea how long it will be until dinner's on the table, so each recipe is marked with a handy symbol:

Timing ▶ = 20 minutes and under

Timing ▶ ▶ = 20–40 minutes

Timing ▶ ▶ ▶ = 40+ minutes

BULK COOKING

Another way to save money is to do your cooking in bulk. Just make a bit extra and put it in the freezer until needed. Don't forget to stock up on some freezer bags or containers, aluminium foil and foil trays to store all your food as individual portions. Good options for bulk cooking include curries, stews, chillies, pasta sauces and soups. You can also freeze small portions of homemade stock in ice cube trays. It's easy then to just take out one at a time to use in your soups and stews – you don't even need to defrost them.

LOVING LEFTOVERS

Just like your gran used to say, 'Waste not, want not'. With a little imagination, today's leftovers can be made into tomorrow's feast. Cooked cold pasta, roasted veg and potatoes can form the basis of salads and tortillas, vegetables can be added to homemade soups or pasta sauces, a few spoons of last night's curry or bolognese sauce will transform a baked potato. Mashed potato could be used to make bubble and squeak, hash browns or fish cakes.

Frying-pan pizza

Tuna pasta bake

Chicken curry

Super Speedy

chicken curry in a hurry

Cost
££

Timing

Serves
4

- 2 tablespoons sunflower oil
- 4 skinless chicken thigh fillets, chopped
- 2 sweet potatoes, peeled and cubed
- 3 tablespoons balti curry paste
- 400 g (13 oz) can chopped tomatoes
- 300 ml (½ pint) chicken stock
- 125 g (4 oz) frozen peas
- small handful of fresh coriander leaves, roughly chopped
- naan bread, to serve

what you do

1. Heat the oil in a large frying pan, add the chicken and sweet potatoes and fry, stirring, over a high heat for 5 minutes.
2. Add the curry paste, tomatoes and stock to the frying pan, bring to the boil, reduce the heat, cover and simmer for 10 minutes. Stir in the peas and cook for a further 5 minutes. Stir in the fresh coriander and serve with warm naan bread.

TIPS Double up on the quantities of this quick curry and freeze half (before you add the coriander) for another meal.

frying-pan pizza

Cost £   Timing   Serves 4

what you need

- 300 g (10 oz) self-raising flour, plus extra for dusting
- 1 teaspoon dried thyme
- 150 ml (¼ pint) warm water
- 1½ tablespoons olive oil
- 6 tablespoons ready-made pizza or tomato pasta sauce
- 50 g (2 oz) can anchovies, drained
- 2 tablespoons capers, drained and rinsed
- 125 g (4 oz) mozzarella cheese, diced
- salt and pepper

what you do

1. Mix the flour in a bowl with the thyme and a generous pinch of salt and pepper. Pour in the warm water and olive oil, and mix to form a soft dough.
2. Divide the dough in half and roll out on a lightly floured surface to fit 2 large nonstick frying pans, approximately 28 cm (11 inches) across. Dust with a little flour. Heat the frying pans over a medium heat and lower the circles of dough carefully into the pans. Cook for about 10 minutes, turning once, until lightly golden.
3. Spread the sauce over the pizza bases and scatter with anchovies and capers. Sprinkle over the mozzarella and cook under a preheated grill for 3–5 minutes, until golden and bubbling. Serve immediately.

huevos rancheros

Cost
£

Timing
🕐

Serves
4

what you need

- 2 tablespoons olive oil
- 1 large onion, diced
- 2 red peppers, deseeded and diced
- 2 garlic cloves, crushed
- ¾ teaspoon dried oregano
- 400 g (13 oz) can chopped tomatoes
- 4 eggs
- 20 g (¾ oz) feta cheese, crumbled
- 4 toasted pitta breads, to serve

what you do

1. Heat the oil in a frying pan over a medium heat, then add the onion, peppers, garlic and oregano and cook for 5 minutes.
2. Add the tomatoes and cook for a further 5 minutes. Pour the tomato mixture into a shallow ovenproof dish and make 4 dips in the mixture.
3. Crack the eggs into the dips, sprinkle with the feta and cook under a preheated hot grill for 3–4 minutes.
4. Serve with toasted pitta breads.

TIPS Eggs – cheap and nutritious student staples – get a Mexican makeover in this dish. Traditionally served for breakfast, it makes a great meal any time.

spaghetti carbonara

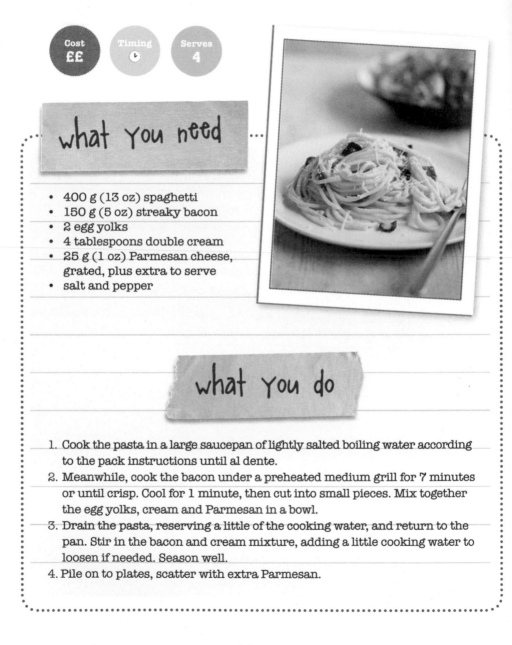

Cost
££

Timing

Serves
4

what you need

- 400 g (13 oz) spaghetti
- 150 g (5 oz) streaky bacon
- 2 egg yolks
- 4 tablespoons double cream
- 25 g (1 oz) Parmesan cheese, grated, plus extra to serve
- salt and pepper

what you do

1. Cook the pasta in a large saucepan of lightly salted boiling water according to the pack instructions until al dente.
2. Meanwhile, cook the bacon under a preheated medium grill for 7 minutes or until crisp. Cool for 1 minute, then cut into small pieces. Mix together the egg yolks, cream and Parmesan in a bowl.
3. Drain the pasta, reserving a little of the cooking water, and return to the pan. Stir in the bacon and cream mixture, adding a little cooking water to loosen if needed. Season well.
4. Pile on to plates, scatter with extra Parmesan.

chicken chilli pasta

Cost
££

Timing
⏱

Serves
4

what You need

- 1 tablespoon sunflower oil
- 500 g (1 lb) chicken mince
- 1 garlic clove, crushed
- 1 teaspoon chilli powder
- ½ teaspoon chilli flakes
- 450 ml (¾ pint) passata
- 1 tablespoon sun-dried tomato pesto
- 375 g (12 oz) spaghetti
- salt and pepper
- freshly grated Parmesan cheese, to serve

what You do

1. Heat the oil in a large frying pan, add the chicken mince and fry over a high heat for 5 minutes, breaking up any clumps.
2. Add the garlic, chilli powder, chilli flakes, passata and pesto. Season with salt and pepper, bring to the boil, then reduce the heat and simmer for 10 minutes.
3. Meanwhile, cook the spaghetti in lightly salted boiling water for 8–10 minutes or until just tender. Drain and toss with the chicken chilli sauce. Serve with plenty of freshly grated Parmesan cheese.

stir-fried vegetable rice

Cost £

Timing

Serves 4

what you need

- 2 tablespoons sunflower oil
- 6 spring onions, cut diagonally into 2.5 cm (1 in) lengths
- 2 garlic cloves, crushed
- 1 teaspoon finely grated fresh root ginger
- 1 red pepper, deseeded and finely chopped
- 1 carrot, peeled and finely diced
- 300 g (10 oz) peas
- 500 g (1 lb) cooked, white long grain rice
- 1 tablespoon dark soy sauce
- 1 tablespoon sweet chilli sauce
- chopped coriander and mint leaves, to garnish

what you do

Heat the oil in a large, nonstick wok or frying pan and add the spring onions, garlic and ginger. Stir-fry for 4-5 minutes and then add the red pepper, carrot and peas. Stir-fry over a high heat for 3-4 minutes. Stir in the rice, soy and sweet chilli sauces and stir-fry for 3-4 minutes or until the rice is heated through and piping hot.

Remove from the heat and serve immediately, garnished with the chopped herbs.

lovely leftovers

You can use up whatever veg you have in the fridge for this stir-fry dish and, if you have any leftover cooked chicken, you can add that too.

tuna pasta bake

what you need

Cost £

Timing ◷

Serves 4

- 300 g (10 oz) pasta shells
- 2 tablespoons olive oil
- 1 onion, finely chopped
- 2 red peppers, cored, deseeded and cubed
- 2 garlic cloves, crushed
- 200 g (7 oz) cherry tomatoes, halved
- 15 g (½ oz) butter
- 50 g (2 oz) fresh breadcrumbs
- 400 g (13 oz) can tuna, drained and flaked
- 125 g (4 oz) mozzarella cheese or Gruyère cheese, grated

what you do

1. Cook the pasta shells in a saucepan of lightly salted boiling water for 8–10 minutes, or according to the packet instructions, until al dente.
2. Meanwhile, heat the oil in a large frying pan. Add the onion and fry gently for 3 minutes. Add the peppers and garlic and carry on frying, stirring frequently, for 5 minutes. Stir in the tomatoes and fry for 1 minute until they are soft.
3. Melt the butter in another pan, toss in the breadcrumbs and stir until all the bread is covered in butter.
4. Drain the pasta, add the pepper and tomato mix, and then the tuna. Mix together, then put in an ovenproof dish.
5. Sprinkle the mozzarella or Gruyère and then the buttered breadcrumbs over the pasta and cook under a medium grill for 3–5 minutes until the cheese has melted and the breadcrumbs are golden.

quick garlicky tomato lentils

Cost
£

Timing
🕐

Serves
4

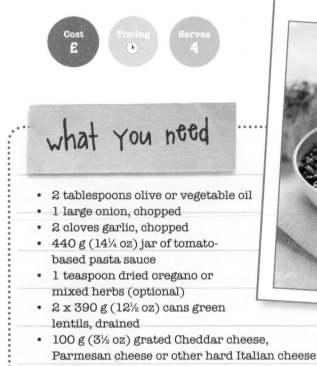

what you need

- 2 tablespoons olive or vegetable oil
- 1 large onion, chopped
- 2 cloves garlic, chopped
- 440 g (14¼ oz) jar of tomato-based pasta sauce
- 1 teaspoon dried oregano or mixed herbs (optional)
- 2 x 390 g (12½ oz) cans green lentils, drained
- 100 g (3½ oz) grated Cheddar cheese, Parmesan cheese or other hard Italian cheese (optional)
- crusty bread or toast, to serve

what you do

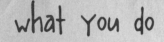

1. Heat the oil in a large frying pan and cook the onion and garlic over a medium heat for 6-7 minutes, stirring frequently, until softened.
2. Add the pasta sauce, herbs and lentils and heat to simmering point.
3. Spoon into bowls. Scatter with cheese, if using, and serve immediately with crusty bread or toast.

thai red pork & bean curry

Cost ££

Timing

Serves 4

what you need

- 2 tablespoons groundnut oil
- 1½ tablespoons Thai red curry paste
- 375 g (12 oz) lean pork, sliced into thin strips
- 100 g (3½ oz) green beans, trimmed and cut in half
- 2 tablespoons Thai fish sauce
- 1 teaspoon caster sugar
- Chinese chives or regular chives, to garnish

what you do

1. Heat the oil in a wok or large frying pan over a medium heat until the oil starts to shimmer, add the curry paste and cook, stirring, until it releases its aroma.
2. Add the pork and beans and stir-fry for 2–3 minutes or until the meat is cooked through and the beans are just tender.
3. Stir in the fish sauce and sugar and serve, garnished with Chinese chives or regular chives.

TIPS Stir-fries are a brilliant way of making a little meat go a long way. Serve with steamed rice for a more filling meal, if you like.

Ratatouille

Beef goulash

Fish curry

One Pot

winter veg & beer broth

Cost £

Timing ⏱ ⏱ ⏱

Serves 6

what you need

- 4 tablespoons olive oil
- 1 onion, chopped
- 2 garlic cloves, crushed
- 1 tablespoon chopped rosemary
- 2 carrots, diced
- 250 g (8 oz) parsnips, diced
- 250 g (8 oz) swede, diced
- 100 g (3½ oz) pearl barley
- 600 ml (1 pint) beer or lager
- 1 litre (1¾ pints) vegetable stock
- 2 tablespoons chopped parsley
- salt and pepper
- crusty bread, to serve

what you do

1. Heat the oil in a large saucepan, add the onion, garlic, rosemary, carrots, parsnips and swede and cook over a low heat, stirring frequently, for 10 minutes.
2. Stir in the barley, beer or lager, stock and salt and pepper and bring to the boil. Reduce the heat, cover and simmer gently for 40–45 minutes until the barley and vegetables are tender.
3. Stir in the parsley and adjust the seasoning. Serve with plenty of crusty bread.

for vegetable & rice soup, omit the beer and increase the stock to 1.5 litres (2½ pints). Replace the barley with an equal quantity of risotto rice. Use 250 g (8 oz) celeriac instead of the parsnips. Continue the recipe as above.

for homemade raita, mix 175 ml (6 fl oz) natural yogurt with 75 g (3 oz) deseeded and grated cucumber, 2 tablespoons chopped mint, a pinch of cumin, and salt and lemon juice to taste.

tandoori chicken

Cost ££　**Timing**　**Serves** 4

what you need

- 4 skinless chicken breast fillets
- 100 ml (3½ fl oz) natural yogurt
- 1 garlic clove, crushed
- 2 teaspoons finely grated fresh root ginger
- 2 tablespoons tandoori curry paste
- 1 onion, cut into wedges
- 2 tablespoons vegetable oil

- 2 tomatoes, quartered
- 15 g (½ oz) butter, cut into small pieces
- salt and pepper

to serve
- lime wedges
- ready-made or homemade raita (see opposite)
- naan breads

what you do

1. Line a baking sheet with foil and set a wire rack on top. Make 3 slashes across each chicken breast. Mix together the yogurt, garlic, ginger and tandoori paste and season well. Rub all over the chicken and leave to marinate for 5–10 minutes.
2. Toss the onion and chicken with the oil, then arrange on the rack. Place in a preheated oven, 230°C (450°F), Gas Mark 8, for 7 minutes.
3. Add the tomatoes, scatter over the butter and return to the oven for a further 5–10 minutes until the chicken is charred and just cooked through. Serve with lime wedges, raita and naan.

veggie goulash with chive dumplings

Cost £

Timing ⏱ ⏱ ⏱

Serves 4

what you do

what you need

- 4 tablespoons olive oil
- 8 baby onions, peeled
- 2 garlic cloves, crushed
- 1 carrot, chopped
- 1 large celery stick, sliced
- 500 g (1 lb) potatoes, cubed
- 1 teaspoon caraway seeds
- 1 teaspoon smoked paprika
- 400 g (13 oz) can chopped tomatoes
- 450 ml (¾ pint) vegetable stock
- salt and pepper

chive dumplings

- 75 g (3 oz) self-raising flour
- ½ teaspoon salt
- 50 g (2 oz) vegetarian suet
- 1 tablespoon chopped chives
- 4–5 tablespoons water

Heat the oil in a large saucepan, add the onions, garlic, carrot, celery, potatoes and caraway seeds and cook over a medium heat, stirring frequently, for 10 minutes. Add the paprika and cook, stirring, for 1 minute.

Stir in the tomatoes, stock and salt and pepper. Bring to the boil, then reduce the heat, cover and simmer gently for 20 minutes.

Make the dumplings. Sift the flour and salt into a bowl and stir in the suet, chives and pepper to taste. Working quickly and lightly, gradually mix in enough of the measurement water to form a soft dough. Divide into 8 equal pieces and roll into balls.

Carefully arrange the dumplings in the stew, leaving gaps between them, cover and simmer for 15 minutes until doubled in size and light and fluffy.

quick one-pot ratatouille

Cost £

Timing ⏱

Serves 4

what you need

- 100 ml (3½ fl oz) olive oil
- 2 onions, chopped
- 1 medium aubergine, cut into bite-sized cubes
- 2 large courgettes, cut into bite-sized pieces
- 1 red pepper, cored, deseeded and cut into bite-sized pieces
- 1 yellow pepper, cored, deseeded and cut into bite-sized pieces
- 2 garlic cloves, crushed
- 400 g (13 oz) can chopped tomatoes
- 4 tablespoons chopped parsley or basil
- salt and pepper

what you do

1. Heat the oil in a large saucepan until very hot, add the onions, aubergine, courgettes, peppers and garlic and cook, stirring constantly, for a few minutes until softened. Add the tomatoes, season to taste with salt and pepper and stir well.
2. Reduce the heat, cover the pan tightly and simmer for 15 minutes until all the vegetables are cooked.
3. Remove from the heat and stir in the chopped parsley or basil before serving.

sausage & bean casserole

what you need

- 1 tablespoon olive oil
- 1 onion, chopped
- 1 garlic clove, crushed
- 1 red pepper, cored, deseeded and chopped
- 8 lean pork sausages, about 400 g (13 oz) in total, quartered
- 2 x 410 g (13½ oz) cans mixed beans, drained and rinsed
- 400 g (13 oz) can chopped tomatoes
- 150 ml (¼ pint) vegetable stock
- 2 tablespoons tomato purée
- 2 tablespoons chopped parsley
- salt and pepper

Cost
££

Timing
◗ ◗

Serves
4

what you do

1. Heat the oil in a saucepan, add the onion, garlic and red pepper and fry for 2–3 minutes until they are beginning to soften.
2. Add the sausages and continue to cook for 5 minutes until browned all over.
3. Crush half of the beans lightly with the back of a fork and add to the pan with the remaining beans, the tomatoes, stock and tomato purée. Season to taste with salt and pepper. Bring to the boil and simmer for 10 minutes. Remove the pan from the heat, stir in the parsley and serve.

pork & sweet potato bake

Cost
££

Timing
◔ ◔

Serves
4

what you need

- 2 tablespoons olive oil
- 1 teaspoon ground coriander
- 4 thick pork chops
- 4 sweet potatoes, peeled and cut into wedges
- 4 garlic cloves, unpeeled
- 2 tablespoons honey
- grated rind and juice of 1 lime
- handful of coriander leaves, chopped
- 1 red chilli, deseeded, if liked, and sliced
- 2 spring onions, sliced
- salt and pepper
- lime wedges, to serve

what you do

1. Place the oil and ground coriander in a small bowl and mix together, then season well. Toss the pork chops, sweet potatoes and garlic in the oil and spread out on a shallow baking tray. Place in a preheated oven, 220°C (425°F), Gas Mark 7, for 10 minutes.
2. Meanwhile, stir together the honey and lime rind and juice in a bowl. Turn the meat and sweet potatoes over, then drizzle over the honey sauce. Return to the oven for a further 5–10 minutes until golden and cooked through.
3. Scatter over the chopped coriander, chilli and spring onions and serve with lime wedges.

pork & tomato rice pot

what you need

Cost **££**

Timing 🕐🕐

Serves **4**

- 3 tablespoons olive oil
- 300 g (10 oz) pork fillet, sliced
- 1 onion, finely chopped
- 3 garlic cloves, finely chopped
- 250 g (8 oz) paella rice
- 2 teaspoons smoked paprika
- 200 g (7 oz) can chopped tomatoes
- 650 ml (1 pint 2 fl oz) hot chicken stock
- 125 g (4 oz) baby spinach leaves
- salt and pepper
- lemon wedges, to serve

TIPS It's worth buying proper short-grain paella rice for this recipe if you can. Long-grain or basmati rice won't absorb the liquid properly.

what you do

1. Heat 1 tablespoon of the oil in a large, deep frying pan over a high heat. Add the pork fillet and cook for 3 minutes until golden and nearly cooked through, then remove from the pan and set aside. Reduce the heat, add the onion to the pan with the remaining oil and cook for 3 minutes until softened, then stir in the garlic and cook for 30 seconds.
2. Add the rice and cook for 1 minute, then add the paprika and tomatoes, bring to the boil and simmer for 2-3 minutes. Pour in the stock, season to taste and cook for a further 12-15 minutes until there is just a little liquid left around the edges of the pan.
3. Lightly fork the spinach through the rice, arrange the pork on top, then cover and continue to cook for 3-4 minutes until cooked through. Serve with lemon wedges for squeezing over.

minestrone soup

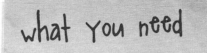

Cost £

Timing ◕ ◕

Serves 4

- 2 tablespoons olive oil
- 1 onion, diced
- 1 garlic clove, crushed
- 2 celery sticks, chopped
- 1 leek, finely sliced
- 1 carrot, chopped
- 400 g (13 oz) can chopped tomatoes
- 600 ml (1 pint) chicken stock or vegetable stock
- 1 courgette, diced
- ½ small green cabbage, shredded
- 1 bay leaf
- 75 g (3 oz) canned haricot beans
- 75 g (3 oz) spaghetti, broken into small pieces, or small pasta shapes
- 1 tablespoon chopped flat leaf parsley
- salt and pepper
- 50 g (2 oz) Parmesan cheese, freshly grated, to serve

1. Heat the oil in a large saucepan. Add the onion, garlic, celery, leek and carrot and sauté over a medium heat, stirring occasionally, for 3 minutes.
2. Add the tomatoes, stock, courgette, cabbage, bay leaf and haricot beans. Bring to the boil, then lower the heat and simmer for 10 minutes.
3. Add the spaghetti and season to taste with salt and pepper. Stir well and cook for a further 8 minutes. Keep stirring, otherwise the soup may stick to the base of the pan.
4. Add the chopped parsley just before serving, and stir well. Ladle into soup bowls and serve with grated Parmesan.

beef goulash

Cost
££

Timing
● ● ●

Serves
8

what you need

- 4 tablespoons olive oil
- 1.5 kg (3 lb) braising steak, cubed
- 2 onions, sliced
- 2 red peppers, cored, deseeded and diced
- 1 tablespoon smoked paprika
- 2 tablespoons chopped marjoram
- 1 teaspoon caraway seeds
- 1 litre (1¾ pints) beef stock
- 5 tablespoons tomato purée
- salt and black pepper

what you do

1. Heat the oil in a flameproof casserole, add the beef, in 3 batches, and cook over a high heat for 5 minutes until browned all over. Remove from the pan with a slotted spoon.
2. Add the onions and red peppers to the pan and cook gently for 10 minutes until softened. Stir in the paprika, marjoram and caraway seeds and cook, stirring, for a further 1 minute.
3. Return the beef to the pan, add the stock, tomato purée and salt and pepper to taste and bring to the boil, stirring. Reduce the heat, cover and simmer gently for 1½-2 hours. You can remove the lid for the final 30 minutes if the sauce needs thickening.

chilli con carne

what you need

- 4 tablespoons olive oil
- 2 red onions, finely chopped
- 6 garlic cloves, finely chopped
- 500 g (1 lb) lean minced beef
- 1 teaspoon ground cumin
- 2 small red peppers, cored, deseeded and diced
- 2 x 400 g (13 oz) cans chopped tomatoes
- 2 tablespoons tomato purée
- 1 tablespoon mild chilli powder
- 400 ml (14 fl oz) beef stock
- 2 x 400 g (13 oz) cans red kidney beans, rinsed and drained
- salt and pepper
- boiled rice, to serve

what you do

1. Heat the oil in a saucepan, add the onion and garlic and cook for 5 minutes until softened. Add the mince and cumin and cook for a further 5-6 minutes, or until browned all over.
2. Stir in the red pepper, tomatoes, tomato purée, chilli powder and stock and bring to the boil, then reduce the heat and simmer gently for 30 minutes.
3. Add the beans and cook for a further 5 minutes. Season to taste and serve with rice.

simple fish curry

Cost ££
Timing ◗ ◗ ◗
Serves 4

what you need

- 40 g (1½ oz) fresh root ginger, grated
- 1 teaspoon ground turmeric
- 2 garlic cloves, crushed
- 2 teaspoons medium curry paste
- 150 ml (¼ pint) natural yogurt
- 625 g (1¼ lb) white fish fillets, skinned
- 2 tablespoons oil
- 1 large onion, sliced
- 1 cinnamon stick, halved
- 2 teaspoons dark muscovado sugar
- 2 bay leaves
- 400 g (13 oz) can chopped tomatoes
- 300 ml (½ pint) fish stock or vegetable stock
- 500 g (1 lb) waxy potatoes, cut into small chunks
- 25 g (1 oz) chopped fresh coriander
- salt and pepper

what you do

1. Mix together the ginger, turmeric, garlic and curry paste in a bowl. Stir in the yogurt until combined. Cut the fish into large pieces and add to the bowl, stirring until coated in the spice mixture.
2. Heat the oil in a large saucepan and gently fry the onion, cinnamon, sugar and bay leaves until the onion is soft. Add the tomatoes, stock and potatoes and bring to the boil. Cook, uncovered, for about 20 minutes until the potatoes are tender and the sauce has thickened.
3. Tip in the fish and spicy yogurt and reduce the heat to its lowest setting. Cook gently for about 10 minutes or until the fish is cooked through. Check the seasoning and stir in the coriander to serve.

TIPS once you've opened a jar of curry paste, don't leave it to rot at the back of the fridge. Use it up in one of the recipes on pages 14, 77 and 90.

Fish pie

Mac & cheese

Toad in the hole

feed-a-cold chicken soup

Cost
££

Timing

Serves
4

what you need

- 1.2 litres (2 pints) hot chicken or vegetable stock
- 1 bay leaf
- 500 g (1 lb) boneless, skinless chicken thighs, trimmed of fat
- 25 g (1 oz) butter
- 1 celery stick, thinly sliced
- 2 leeks, trimmed, cleaned and thinly sliced
- 2 carrots, thinly sliced
- 125 g (4 oz) mushrooms, sliced
- 1 garlic clove, chopped
- 75 g (3 oz) frozen sweetcorn
- 75 g (3 oz) angel hair pasta
- salt and pepper
- chilli oil, to drizzle (optional)
- chopped parsley, to garnish

Bring the stock and bay leaf to the boil in a saucepan and add the chicken. Cover loosely and simmer for 20 minutes, until cooked and tender. Scoop out the meat with a slotted spoon and set aside to cool slightly, reserving the stock. Meanwhile, melt the butter in a large pan and cook the celery, leeks and carrots for 7–8 minutes, until softened. Add the mushrooms and garlic and cook for further 3–4 minutes.

Pour in the reserved stock, add the corn and return to the boil. Season to taste. Tip the pasta into the pan and cook for 3–4 minutes, or until al dente.

Shred the chicken and add to the broth. Ladle into bowls and serve drizzled with chilli oil, if liked, and garnished with chopped parsley and freshly ground pepper.

beef stew with garlic bread topping

what you need

Cost
££

Timing

Serves
4

- 2 tablespoons olive oil
- 400 g (13 oz) beef steak, cut into chunks
- 1 onion, sliced
- 1 carrot, sliced
- 1 celery stick, sliced
- 1 teaspoon tomato purée
- 2 teaspoons plain flour
- handful of chopped thyme
- 100 ml (3½ fl oz) red wine
- 200 ml (7 fl oz) hot beef stock
- ½ ready-made garlic bread baguette, sliced
- salt and pepper

what you do

1. Heat half the oil in a flameproof casserole dish over a high heat. Add the beef and cook for 2-3 minutes until golden, then remove from the pan and set aside. Add the remaining oil and cook the onion, carrot and celery for 5 minutes until softened.
2. Stir in the tomato purée, flour and thyme, then pour in the wine and cook for 2-3 minutes until reduced by half. Add the stock and simmer for 15 minutes, then return the meat to the pan.
3. Arrange the garlic bread slices on top of the stew, then cook under a preheated hot grill for 3 minutes until the bread is golden and crisp.

toad in the hole

Cost ££

Timing

Serves 4

what you need

- 125 g (4 oz) plain flour
- 1 egg
- 300 ml (½ pint) milk or equal mixture of milk and water
- 500 g (1 lb) pork sausages
- 8 rindless bacon rashers
- 2 tablespoons vegetable oil
- salt and pepper
- baked beans, to serve (optional)

TIPS Serve this with Irish champ. Cook 1.5 Kg (3 lb) potatoes in lightly salted boiling water for 20 minutes, drain, return to the pan and mash. Beat in 150 ml (1/4 pint) milk, 3 chopped spring onions, 50 g (2 oz) butter and season.

what you do

1. Put the flour and a dash of salt and pepper in a bowl, then crack in the egg. Slowly whisk in the milk or milk-and-water mixture until the batter is smooth and frothy.
2. Separate the sausages from each other. Stretch each rasher of bacon by laying it on a chopping board and running the flat edge of a knife along the rasher until it is half as long again. Wrap a rasher of bacon around each sausage.
3. Pour the oil into a roasting tin and add the bacon-wrapped sausages, keeping them spaced apart. Roast in a preheated oven, 220°C (425°F), Gas Mark 7, for 5 minutes until sizzling. Whisk the batter again.
4. Take the roasting tin out of the oven and quickly pour in the batter, making sure that the sausages are still spaced apart. Return the tin to the oven and cook for about 20 minutes until the batter is risen and golden and the sausages are cooked through. Serve with baked beans or Irish champ (see Tips), if liked.

mustard rarebit

what you need

- 25 g (1 oz) butter
- 4 spring onions, thinly sliced
- 250 g (8 oz) Cheddar or Red Leicester cheese, grated
- 50 ml (2 fl oz) beer
- 2 teaspoons mustard
- 4 slices of wholemeal bread
- pepper
- salad to serve (optional)

what you do

1. Heat the butter in a frying pan, add the spring onions and fry for 5 minutes or until softened.
2. Reduce the heat to low and stir in the cheese, beer and mustard. Season well with pepper, then stir slowly for 3–4 minutes or until the cheese has melted.
3. Meanwhile, toast the bread lightly on both sides and place on a grill pan. Pour the cheese mixture over the toast and cook under a preheated hot grill for 1 minute or until bubbling and golden. Serve with a salad, if liked.

mac & cheese with spinach

Cost ££

Timing ◑◑

Serves 4

what you need

- 300 g (10 oz) macaroni
- 350 g (11½ oz) baby spinach leaves
- 50 g (2 oz) butter
- 50 g (2 oz) plain flour
- 750 ml (1¼ pints) milk
- 150 g (5 oz) Taleggio or fontina cheese, chopped
- 2 teaspoons wholegrain mustard
- 1 teaspoon Dijon mustard
- 8 cherry tomatoes, halved
- 50 g (2 oz) fresh white breadcrumbs
- 25 g (2 oz) Cheddar cheese, grated
- salt and pepper

what you do

1. Cook the macaroni in a large saucepan of lightly salted boiling water for 8–10 minutes, or according to the packet instructions, until al dente.
2. Add the spinach to the pan and cook for 1 minute until wilted. Drain well and place in a 1.5 litre (2½ pint) ovenproof dish.
3. Meanwhile, place the butter, flour and milk in a saucepan and whisk constantly over a medium heat until the sauce boils and thickens. Simmer for 2–3 minutes until you have a smooth glossy sauce, then reduce the heat to low and stir in the Taleggio or fontina and mustards. Season to taste with salt and pepper and cook gently until the cheese has melted.
4. Pour the sauce over the macaroni and spinach, scatter over the tomatoes and then sprinkle with the breadcrumbs and Cheddar. Bake in a preheated oven, 200°C (400°F), Gas Mark 6, for 20 minutes until golden and bubbling.

fish pie

- 750 g (1½ lb) floury potatoes, cut into chunks
- 2 eggs (optional)
- 400 ml (14 fl oz) full-fat milk
- 50 g (2 oz) plain flour
- 100 g (3½ oz) butter
- 2 tablespoons chopped parsley
- 25 g (1 oz) watercress, roughly chopped (optional)
- 200 g (7 oz) raw peeled king prawns
- 390 g (12¾ oz) shop-bought fish pie mixture (available from the chilled section of supermarkets), or use bite-sized chunks of salmon, white fish fillet and smoked haddock
- 3 tablespoons crème fraîche
- 75 g (3 oz) Cheddar cheese, grated
- salt and pepper

what you do

1. Cook the potatoes in a pan of lightly salted boiling water for around 10–12 minutes, until tender.
2. Hard-boil the eggs, if using, in a pan of simmering water for about 8 minutes. Drain and hold under cold running water. Once cool enough to handle, remove the shells and cut the eggs into wedges.
3. Place the milk, flour and half the butter in a saucepan and bring slowly to the boil, stirring constantly with a balloon whisk, until thick and smooth. Simmer for 1–2 minutes, then season lightly and take off the heat.
4. Stir the parsley, watercress (if using), prawns, fish and egg into the sauce, then transfer to an ovenproof dish.
5. Drain the potatoes and mash them with the crème fraîche and the remaining butter. Season to taste, then spoon over the fish mixture and scatter with the grated cheese. Place the pie in a preheated oven, 220°C (425°F), Gas Mark 7, for 12–15 minutes, until golden and bubbling and the fish is cooked.

barbecue bacon burger & cheesy chips

Cost **££** Timing ⏱ Serves **2**

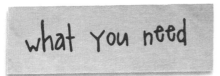

- 250 g (8 oz) oven chips
- 2 tablespoons vegetable oil
- 4 slices of smoked streaky bacon
- 300 g (10 oz) minced beef
- 1 teaspoon dried oregano
- ½ red onion, very finely chopped (optional)
- 50 g (2 oz) crumbled blue cheese
- 50 g (2 oz) very finely grated Cheddar cheese
- salt and pepper

to serve
- barbecue sauce
- 2 large burger buns, split and toasted

what you do

1. Arrange the chips in a single layer on a large baking sheet and cook in a preheated oven, 220°C (425°F), Gas Mark 7, for 15–18 minutes or according to packet instructions until crisp and golden.
2. Meanwhile, heat the vegetable oil in a medium-sized frying pan and cook the bacon over a medium heat for 4–5 minutes until golden. Remove from the pan and keep warm.
3. While the bacon is cooking, mix the minced beef in a bowl with the oregano, onion, blue cheese and a pinch each of salt and pepper. Shape into 2 burgers and cook in the pan a medium heat for 3–5 minutes on each side until cooked through but still juicy.
4. Assemble the burgers in burger buns with the frazzled bacon and a dollop of barbecue sauce, adding other fillings of your choice if liked.
5. Remove the chips from the oven, tip into a bowl and scatter with the grated Cheddar cheese.

sausage & onion with mustard mash

Cost
££

Timing

Serves
4

- 8 sausages
- 4 red onions, cut into wedges
- 2 leeks, thickly sliced
- 3–4 rosemary sprigs
- 2 tablespoons olive oil
- 875 g (1¾ lb) potatoes, peeled and cut into chunks
- 50 g (2 oz) butter
- 2–3 tablespoons wholegrain mustard
- pepper

what you do

1. Place the sausages, onions and leeks in a large roasting tin, toss with the rosemary and oil and season with pepper. Roast in a preheated oven, 200°C (400°F), Gas Mark 6, for 25 minutes, tossing a couple of times during the cooking time.
2. Meanwhile, cook the potatoes in a pan of lightly salted boiling water for 12–15 minutes, until tender.
3. Drain the potatoes, return to the pan and mash with the butter until smooth. Stir in the wholegrain mustard.
4. Divide the mustard mash between 4 plates. Spoon over the sausages, roast vegetables and any juices from the roasting tin.

cauliflower cheese

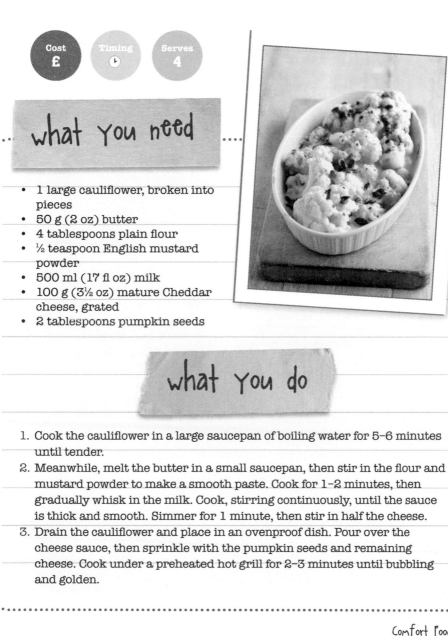

Cost £

Timing ⏱

Serves 4

what you need

- 1 large cauliflower, broken into pieces
- 50 g (2 oz) butter
- 4 tablespoons plain flour
- ½ teaspoon English mustard powder
- 500 ml (17 fl oz) milk
- 100 g (3½ oz) mature Cheddar cheese, grated
- 2 tablespoons pumpkin seeds

what you do

1. Cook the cauliflower in a large saucepan of boiling water for 5–6 minutes until tender.
2. Meanwhile, melt the butter in a small saucepan, then stir in the flour and mustard powder to make a smooth paste. Cook for 1–2 minutes, then gradually whisk in the milk. Cook, stirring continuously, until the sauce is thick and smooth. Simmer for 1 minute, then stir in half the cheese.
3. Drain the cauliflower and place in an ovenproof dish. Pour over the cheese sauce, then sprinkle with the pumpkin seeds and remaining cheese. Cook under a preheated hot grill for 2–3 minutes until bubbling and golden.

shepherd's pie

Cost ££

Timing ● ● ●

Serves 4–6

what you need

- 1 tablespoon olive oil
- 1 onion, finely chopped
- 1 carrot, diced
- 1 celery stick, diced
- 1 tablespoon chopped thyme
- 500 g (1 lb) minced lamb
- 400 g (13 oz) can chopped tomatoes
- 4 tablespoons tomato purée
- 750 g (1½ lb) floury potatoes, such as Desiree, peeled and cubed
- 50 g (2 oz) butter
- 3 tablespoons milk
- 75 g (3 oz) Cheddar cheese, grated
- salt and pepper

what you do

1. Heat the oil in a saucepan, add the onion, carrot, celery and thyme and cook gently for 10 minutes until soft and golden.
2. Add the minced lamb and cook over a high heat, breaking up with a wooden spoon, for 5 minutes until browned. Add the tomatoes, tomato purée and salt and pepper to taste. Bring to the boil, then reduce the heat, cover and simmer for 30 minutes.
3. Remove the lid and cook for a further 15 minutes until thickened.
4. Meanwhile, put the potatoes in a large saucepan of lightly salted water and bring to the boil. Reduce the heat and simmer for 15–20 minutes until really tender. Drain well and return to the pan. Mash in the butter, milk and half the cheese and season to taste with salt and pepper.
5. Spoon the minced lamb mixture into an ovenproof dish and carefully spoon the mash over the top, spreading over the surface of the filling. Fork the top of the mash and scatter over the remaining cheese. Bake in a preheated oven, 190°C (375°F), Gas Mark 5, for 20–25 minutes until bubbling and golden.

kedgeree with poached eggs

Cost ££   **Timing** ⏱⏱   **Serves** 4

what you need

- 50 g (2 oz) butter
- 6 spring onions, chopped
- 2 tablespoons mild curry powder
- 300 g (10 oz) basmati rice
- 300 ml (10 fl oz) chicken stock
- 250 g (8 oz) smoked haddock, skinned and cut into chunks
- 200 ml (7 fl oz) whipping cream
- 3 tablespoons chopped parsley
- 1 tablespoon white wine vinegar or malt vinegar
- 4 very fresh large eggs
- salt and pepper

to serve
- 1 lemon, cut into wedges
- mango chutney

TIPS Instead of poaching the eggs, you can hard-boil them, then peel and roughly chop them and stir gently through the kedgeree.

what you do

Melt the butter in a large saucepan over a medium heat. Add the spring onions and fry until soft. Add the curry powder and fry for a further minute until fragrant. Add the rice to the pan and stir well.

Pour in the stock and bring to the boil, then simmer for 7–10 minutes, or until the rice is just cooked. Add the smoked haddock, cream and parsley. Cook for a further 2 minutes until the fish is cooked and firm. Season with salt and pepper.

Bring a large saucepan of water to the boil. Add the vinegar and a pinch of salt. Whisk the water around the pan, then crack the first egg into the centre of the spiral of water. Reduce the heat and simmer for 2–3 minutes until the white of the egg is set but the yolk is still soft. Remove from the pan using a slotted spoon and plunge into a bowl of ice-cold water to stop the cooking process. Repeat with the remaining eggs. Once all the eggs are cooked, bring the water back up to the simmer and return the eggs to the water for 1 minute to warm through. Serve the hot kedgeree with the poached eggs, a wedge of lemon and some mango chutney.

Quinoa porridge

Baked cod

Curried cauliflower

Good for You

crunchy honey yogurt

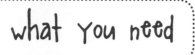

Cost ££

Timing 🕐

Serves 6

what you need

- 500 g (1 lb) Greek yogurt
- 125 g (4 oz) strawberries, quartered
  topping
- 50 g (2 oz) flaked almonds
- 50 g (2 oz) pumpkin seeds
- 50 g (2 oz) sunflower seeds
- 3 tablespoons sesame seeds
- 50 g (2 oz) oats
- 6 tablespoons golden caster sugar
- 4 tablespoons clear honey, plus extra to drizzle (optional)

TIPS Store any leftover topping in an airtight container. It will keep for up to 2 weeks.

what you do

1. Mix the almonds, seeds, oats and sugar in a large bowl. Line a large baking sheet with nonstick baking paper, then pour the nut and seed mixture over. Lightly shake the baking sheet to level the ingredients.
2. Drizzle the honey in thin streams over the top, then place under a preheated medium grill for 3–4 minutes until the sugar begins to caramelize and the nuts and seeds turn golden brown. Remove from the grill and set aside to cool and harden. Place the hardened nuts and seeds in a polythene bag and bash with a rolling pin to crush into a crunchy topping.
3. Spoon the yogurt into a bowl and fold in the strawberries. Divide between bowls and sprinkle with the topping. Drizzle with more honey, if liked.

apple & yogurt muesli

Cost
£

Timing
🕐

Serves
4

what you need

- 400 g (13 oz) fruit and nut muesli
- 2 dessert apples, such as Granny Smiths, peeled and coarsely grated
- 450 ml (¾ pint) chilled apple juice
- 250 g (8 oz) fat-free Greek yogurt with honey
- 2 teaspoons golden linseeds (optional)
- clear honey (optional)

what you do

1. Place the muesli in a bowl and mix with the apples. Pour over the apple juice, stir well to combine and leave to soak for 5–6 minutes.
2. Divide the soaked muesli into bowls and spoon the yogurt on top of each one. Scatter over the linseeds, if using, and serve drizzled with some clear honey, if liked.

quinoa porridge with raspberries

Cost £

Timing 🕐🕐

Serves 2

what you need

- 600 ml (1 pint) milk
- 100 g (3½ oz) quinoa
- 2 tablespoons caster sugar
- ½ teaspoon ground cinnamon
- 125 g (4 oz) fresh raspberries
- 2 tablespoons mixed seeds, such as sunflower, linseed, pumpkin and hemp
- 2 tablespoons clear honey

what you do

1. Bring the milk to the boil in a small saucepan. Add the quinoa and return to the boil. Reduce the heat to low, cover and simmer for about 15 minutes until three-quarters of the milk has been absorbed.
2. Stir the sugar and cinnamon into the pan, re-cover and cook for 8–10 minutes or until almost all the milk has been absorbed and the quinoa is tender.
3. Spoon the porridge into bowls, then top with the raspberries, sprinkle over the seeds and drizzle with the honey. Serve immediately.

TIPS A mega-healthy way to start the day, this alternative to traditional porridge is packed with healthy oils, protein and antioxidants.

greek salad

Cost £

Timing ⏱

Serves 2

- ½ cucumber
- 4 plum tomatoes
- 1 red pepper
- 1 green pepper
- ½ red onion
- 60 g (2¼ oz) pitted Kalamata olives
- 50 g (2 oz) feta cheese, diced

dressing
- 4 tablespoons olive oil
- 1 tablespoon chopped parsley
- salt and pepper

lovely leftovers

Any leftover salad can be the basis of another meal – serve it with toasted pitta bread, a dollop of tzatziki or hummus, or try it with the tzatziki toasts on page 111.

Cut the cucumber and tomatoes into 1–2 cm (½–¾ inch) chunks and put them in a large salad bowl. Cut the flesh from the peppers and carefully remove the ribs and the seeds. Cut the pepper flesh into thin strips and put them in the bowl with the cucumbers and tomatoes. Finely slice the red onion and add to the bowl with the olives. Make the dressing by whisking the oil and parsley. Season to taste with salt and pepper. Pour the dressing over the salad and toss carefully. Transfer to bowls, scatter some feta evenly over each bowl and serve.

chicken couscous salad

Cost ££

Timing

Serves 4

what you need

- 4 boneless, skinless chicken breasts, each about 125 g (4 oz)
- 300 g (10 oz) couscous
- 300 ml (½ pint) hot chicken stock
- 1 pomegranate
- rind and juice of 1 orange
- small bunch of coriander
- small bunch of mint
  marinade
- 1½ tablespoons curry paste (tikka masala)
- 5 tablespoons natural yogurt
- 1 teaspoon olive oil
- 2 tablespoons lemon juice

1. Make a marinade by mixing the curry paste, yogurt and oil. Put the chicken in a non-metallic dish, cover with half the marinade and leave for at least 1 hour.
2. Put the couscous in a bowl, add the hot stock, cover and leave for 8 minutes.
3. Meanwhile, cut the pomegranate in half and remove the seeds. Add them to the couscous with the orange rind and juice.
4. Remove the chicken from the marinade, reserving the marinade, and transfer to a foil-lined baking sheet. Cook in a preheated oven, 190°C (375°F), Gas Mark 5, for 6–7 minutes, then transfer to a preheated hot grill and cook for 2 minutes until caramelized. Cover with foil and leave to rest for 5 minutes.
5. Roughly chop the coriander and mint, reserving some whole coriander leaves for garnish, and add to the couscous. Thinly slice the chicken. Spoon the couscous on to plates and add the chicken. Thin the reserved marinade with the lemon juice and drizzle over the couscous. Garnish with the reserved coriander leaves and serve immediately.

roasted veggie & quinoa salad

what you need

- 3 courgettes, cut into chunks
- 2 red peppers, cored, deseeded and cut into chunks
- 2 red onions, cut into wedges
- 1 large aubergine, cut into chunks
- 3 garlic cloves, peeled
- 3 tablespoons olive oil
- 150 g (5 oz) quinoa
- 2 tablespoons green pesto or sun-dried tomato paste
- 1 tablespoon balsamic vinegar
- 75 g (3 oz) rocket leaves

what you do

1. Put all the vegetables and garlic on a large baking sheet and drizzle over the olive oil. Place in a preheated oven, 220°C (425°F), Gas Mark 7, for 20–25 minutes until tender and beginning to char.
2. Cook the quinoa, meanwhile, in a saucepan of boiling water according to the pack instructions, then drain well.
3. Whisk together the pesto or tomato paste and balsamic vinegar in a small bowl. Place the roasted vegetables, rocket and quinoa in a large bowl and stir in the dressing. Serve warm.

lovely leftovers

Equally delicious served cold, any leftovers can be popped in a lidded container for a quick portable lunch.

niçoise salad

Cost £

Timing ◑◑

Serves 4

what you need

- 400 g (13 oz) small potatoes
- 200 g (7 oz) green beans, trimmed
- 5 large plum tomatoes
- 2 tablespoons chopped parsley, plus extra leaves for garnish
- 60 g (2¼ oz) pitted black olives
- 2 tablespoons lemon juice
- 2–3 tablespoons olive oil
- 4 large, soft-poached eggs
- salt and pepper

what you do

1. Cook the potatoes in lightly salted boiling water, leave them to cool and halve them. Meanwhile, bring a large saucepan of lightly salted water to the boil, add the trimmed green beans and cook for 1–2 minutes until bright green and still firm to the touch. Refresh in cold water, drain and transfer to a large salad bowl.
2. Core the tomatoes and cut each one into 6 pieces. Add the tomatoes and chopped parsley to the beans with the potatoes, olives, lemon juice and oil. Season to taste with salt and pepper.
3. Transfer the salad to plates and top each one with a poached egg cut in half and a drizzle of olive oil. Garnish with the reserved parsley leaves and serve.

smoked mackerel superfood salad

Cost **££**

Timing

Serves **4**

what you need

- 500 g (1 lb) butternut squash, peeled, deseeded and cut into 1 cm (½ inch) cubes
- 4 tablespoons olive oil
- 1 teaspoon cumin seeds
- 1 head of broccoli, cut into florets
- 200 g (7 oz) frozen or fresh peas
- 3 tablespoons quinoa
- 4 tablespoons mixed seeds
- 2 smoked mackerel fillets
- juice of 1 lemon
- ½ teaspoon honey
- ½ teaspoon Dijon mustard
- 100 g (3½ oz) red cabbage, shredded
- 4 tomatoes, chopped
- 4 cooked beetroot, cut into wedges
- 20 g (¾ oz) radish sprouts

what you do

1. Place the squash in a roasting tin and sprinkle with 1 tablespoon of the olive oil and the cumin seeds. Place in a preheated oven, 200°C (400°F), Gas Mark 6, for 15–18 minutes until tender. Leave to cool slightly.
2. Meanwhile, cook the broccoli in boiling water for 4–5 minutes until tender, adding the peas 3 minutes before the end of the cooking time. Remove with a slotted spoon and refresh under cold running water, then drain. Cook the quinoa in the broccoli water for 15 minutes, then drain and leave to cool slightly.
3. Heat a nonstick frying pan over a medium-low heat and dry-fry the seeds, stirring frequently, until golden brown and toasted; set aside. Heat the mackerel fillets according to the pack instructions. Skin and break into flakes.
4. Whisk together the remaining olive oil, lemon juice, honey and mustard in a small bowl. Toss together all the ingredients, except the radish sprouts, with the dressing in a large bowl. Serve topped with the sprouts.

thai red curry chicken soup

Cost **££**

Timing 🕐

Serves **4**

what you need

- 1 tablespoon sunflower oil
- 2 skinless chicken breast fillets, cut into strips
- 375 g (12 oz) butternut squash, peeled, deseeded and cut into small pieces
- 1 red pepper, cored, deseeded and cut into small pieces
- 1 tablespoon Thai red curry paste
- 400 ml (14 fl oz) can reduced-fat coconut milk
- 600 ml (1 pint) chicken stock
- 175 g (6 oz) green beans, halved
- small handful of fresh coriander leaves, roughly chopped

what you do

1. Heat the oil in a large saucepan, add the chicken, butternut squash and red pepper and fry over a high heat for 5 minutes.
2. Add the curry paste, fry for 1 minute then stir in the coconut milk, stock and green beans. Bring to the boil, reduce the heat, cover and simmer for 10 minutes until the chicken and vegetables are cooked. Stir in the fresh coriander and serve.

butter bean & vegetable soup

what you need

- 1 tablespoon olive oil
- 2 teaspoons smoked paprika
- 1 celery stick, sliced
- 2 carrots, sliced
- 1 leek, trimmed, cleaned and sliced
- 600 ml (1 pint) vegetable stock
- 400 g (13 oz) can chopped tomatoes
- 400 g (13 oz) can butter beans, drained and rinsed
- 2 teaspoons chopped rosemary
- salt and pepper
- 50 g (2 oz) Parmesan cheese, grated, to serve

Cost
£

Timing
◑ ◑

Serves
4

what you do

1. Heat the oil in a large saucepan, add the paprika, celery, carrots and leek and cook over a medium heat for 3–4 minutes until the vegetables are slightly softened.
2. Pour over the stock and tomatoes and add the butter beans and rosemary. Season to taste with salt and pepper and bring to the boil, then cover and simmer for 15 minutes or until the vegetables are just tender.
3. Ladle into bowls and sprinkle with the cheese and freshly ground pepper.

pasta with lentils, kale & onions

Cost
£

Timing
🕐

Serves
4

what you need

- 2 tablespoons olive oil
- 2 onions, cut into rings
- pinch of dried chilli flakes
- 2 garlic cloves, finely sliced
- 50 g (2 oz) Puy lentils, rinsed and drained
- 400 g (13 oz) tricolore fusilli
- 125 g (4 oz) kale, chopped
- salt and pepper

what you do

1. Heat the oil in a nonstick frying pan, add the onions and chilli flakes, season well and cook over a low heat for 15 minutes or until very soft and lightly browned. Add the garlic and cook for a further couple of minutes.
2. Meanwhile, cook the lentils in a saucepan of lightly salted simmering water according to the pack instructions, then drain.
3. While the onions and lentils are cooking, cook the pasta in a large saucepan of salted boiling water according to the pack instructions until al dente. Add the kale 3 minutes before the end of the cooking time and cook until tender. Drain, reserving a little of the cooking water, and return to the pan. Toss together with the lentils, adding a little cooking water to loosen if needed.
4. Spoon into bowls and scatter with the caramelized onions.

sweet potatoes with tomato salsa

 Cost
£

 Timing

Serves
4

what you do

1. Scrub the potatoes and place in a small roasting tin. Prick with a fork, drizzle with the oil and sprinkle with a little salt. Put in a preheated oven, 200°C (400°F), Gas Mark 6, for 45 minutes until tender.
2. Meanwhile, make the salsa. Finely chop the tomatoes and mix with the onion, celery, coriander, lime juice and sugar in a bowl.
3. Halve the potatoes and fluff up the flesh with a fork. Sprinkle with the cheese and top with the salsa. Serve with a green salad.

what you need

- 4 large sweet potatoes, about 275 g (9 oz) each
- 2 tablespoons olive oil
- 100 g (3½ oz) Emmental or Cheddar cheese, grated
- salt

tomato salsa
- 4 large tomatoes
- 1 small red onion, finely chopped
- 2 celery sticks, finely chopped
- handful of coriander, chopped
- 4 tablespoons lime juice
- 4 teaspoons caster sugar
- green salad, to serve

TIPS There are plenty of easy toppings for the humble but healthy sweet potato. Try feta and olives, tinned tuna mixed with natural yogurt or steamed broccoli and Cheddar...

egg-filled mushrooms on toast

Cost
£

Timing

Serves
4

what you do

what you need

- 25 g (1 oz) butter
- 4 eggs, beaten
- ½ tablespoon chives, chopped
- 1 tablespoon olive oil
- 4 portobello mushrooms
- 4 slices of bread, toasted
- 2 tomatoes, chopped
- 2 spring onions, thinly sliced
- salt and pepper

1. Melt the butter in a small frying pan. Pour in the eggs and chives, season with salt and pepper and cook for 4–5 minutes, stirring occasionally.
2. Meanwhile, heat the oil in a frying pan and cook the mushrooms for 3–4 minutes on each side.
3. Mix together the tomatoes and spring onions.
4. Place the toast on plates and top with the mushrooms. Drizzle over any pan juices. Spoon the scrambled egg into the mushrooms and serve sprinkled with the tomato and spring onion mixture.

chicken & vegetable stir-fry

Cost ££

Timing ⏱

Serves 4

what you need

- 2 tablespoons coconut oil
- 3-cm (1¼-inch) piece of fresh root ginger, peeled and finely diced
- 2 garlic cloves, crushed
- 1 onion, chopped
- 450 g (14½ oz) chicken breast fillets, cut into strips
- 125 g (4 oz) mushrooms, quartered
- 300 g (10 oz) broccoli florets
- 125 g (4 oz) curly kale, chopped
- 1–2 tablespoons soy sauce
- 2 tablespoons sesame seeds

what you do

1. Heat the oil in a wok or large frying pan until hot, add the ginger, garlic and onion and stir-fry for 30 seconds. Add the chicken and stir-fry for a further 2–3 minutes.
2. Add the vegetables, then sprinkle over the soy sauce. Stir-fry for 1–2 minutes, then cover and steam for a further 4–5 minutes until the vegetables are tender and the chicken is cooked through.
3. Serve sprinkled with the sesame seeds.

TIPS This quick and easy stir-fry includes 'queen of greens' kale, plus broccoli which is high in choline to help boost the growth of brain cells.

curried cauliflower with chickpeas

what you need

- 2 tablespoons olive oil
- 1 onion, chopped
- 2 garlic cloves, crushed
- 4 tablespoons medium curry paste
- 1 small cauliflower, divided into florets
- 375 ml (13 fl oz) vegetable stock
- 4 tomatoes, roughly chopped
- 400 g (13 oz) canned chickpeas, drained and rinsed
- 2 tablespoons mango chutney
- salt and pepper
- 4 tablespoons chopped coriander, to garnish
- whisked natural yogurt, to serve (optional)

Cost
£

Timing

Serves
4

what you do

1. Heat the oil in a saucepan, add the onion and garlic and cook until the onion is soft and starting to brown. Stir in the curry paste, add the cauliflower and stock and bring to the boil. Reduce the heat, cover tightly and simmer for 10 minutes.

2. Add the tomatoes, chickpeas and chutney and cook, uncovered, for a further 10 minutes. Season to taste with salt and pepper. Serve garnished with coriander and drizzled with a little whisked yogurt, if liked.

baked cod with tomatoes & olives

Cost
££

Timing

Serves
4

what you need

- 250 g (8 oz) cherry tomatoes, halved
- 100 g (3½ oz) pitted black olives
- 2 tablespoons capers in brine, drained
- 4 thyme sprigs, plus extra for garnish
- 4 cod fillets, about 175 g (6 oz) each
- 2 tablespoons olive oil
- 2 tablespoons balsamic vinegar
- salt and pepper
- green leaf salad, to serve

TIPS Serve with a mixed leaf salad with a tangy dressing. For the dressing, whisk together 1 teaspoon Dijon mustard, 2 tablespoons white wine vinegar, 4 tablespoons olive oil and salt and pepper.

what you do

1. Combine the tomatoes, olives, capers and thyme sprigs in a roasting tin. Nestle the cod fillets in the pan, drizzle over the oil and balsamic vinegar and season to taste with salt and pepper.
2. Bake in a preheated oven, 200°C (400°F), Gas Mark 6, for 15 minutes.
3. Transfer the fish, tomatoes and olives to plates. Spoon the pan juices over the fish. Serve immediately with a mixed green leaf salad.

Roast chicken

Cheese fondue

Meatballs with tomato sauce

Food for Friends

goats' cheese
& chive soufflés

what you need

- 25 g (1 oz) unsalted butter
- 2 tablespoons plain flour
- 250 ml (8 fl oz) milk
- 100 g (3½ oz) soft goats' cheese
- 3 eggs, separated
- 2 tablespoons chopped chives
- salt and pepper

Cost
££

Timing

Serves
4

what you do

1. Melt the butter in a saucepan, add the flour and cook over a low heat, stirring, for 30 seconds. Remove the pan from the heat and gradually stir in the milk until smooth. Return to the heat and cook, stirring constantly, until the mixture thickens. Cook for 1 minute.
2. Leave to cool slightly, then beat in the goats' cheese, egg yolks, chives, and salt and pepper to taste. Whisk the egg whites in a large, perfectly clean bowl, until soft peaks form. Fold the egg whites into the cheese mixture. Spoon the mixture into 4 greased, individual soufflé ramekins and set on a baking sheet.
3. Bake in a preheated oven, 200°C (400°F), Gas Mark 6, for 15–18 minutes until risen and golden. Serve immediately.

asparagus, pea & mint risotto

Cost
££

Timing
⊙ ⊙ ⊙

Serves
4

what you need

- 500 g (1 lb) asparagus spears
- 1 litre (1¾ pints) vegetable stock
- 50 g (2 oz) butter
- 1 onion, finely chopped
- 300 g (10 oz) arborio, carnaroli or vialone nano rice
- 150 ml (¼ pint) dry white wine
- 100 g (3½ oz) shelled fresh or frozen peas
- 4 tablespoons freshly grated Parmesan cheese, plus extra to serve
- handful of mint leaves, roughly chopped

Cut the asparagus in half, at an angle, separating the tips from the thicker stalks. Reserve the tips. Put the stalks in a saucepan with the stock and bring to the boil. Boil for 5 minutes, then reduce to a simmer. Remove the stalks with a slotted spoon and process to a purée in a food processor or blender. If you don't have a blender, mash the asparagus stalks well with a potato masher.

Melt half the butter in a heavy-based saucepan over a low heat. Add the onion and cook for 10 minutes until softened. Add the rice and cook, stirring, for 1 minute. Add the wine and cook, stirring, until absorbed. Stir in the puréed asparagus.

Add 2 ladlefuls of the simmering stock. Slowly simmer, stirring constantly, until the stock has been absorbed and the rice parts when a wooden spoon is run through it. Add another ladleful of stock and continue to cook, stirring and adding the stock in ladlefuls, reserving 2 ladlefuls, for 16–18 minutes until the rice is creamy and almost tender to the bite.

Add the peas and the reserved asparagus tips and stock and continue cooking until the stock is almost absorbed. Remove from the heat and stir in the Parmesan, mint and remaining butter. Stir vigorously for 15 seconds. Cover with a tight-fitting lid and leave to stand for 2 minutes. Serve immediately with extra Parmesan cheese.

classic cheese fondue

what you need

- 1 garlic clove, peeled and halved
- 200 ml (7 fl oz) dry white wine
- 2 teaspoons vinegar or lemon juice
- 1½ tablespoons cornflour
- 4 tablespoons kirsch, brandy, vodka or dry white wine
- 750 g (1½ lb) mixture of grated cheese (such as Emmental, Gruyère and mature Cheddar cheese)
- selection of dippers, such as cubes of crusty bread, raw vegetables (carrot and celery sticks, broccoli and cauliflower florets, halved mushrooms, cherry tomatoes), cooked sausages, pickled onions, cornichons and new potatoes, to serve

what you do

1. Rub the cut side of the garlic all over the inside of a saucepan, then discard. Pour in the wine and vinegar or lemon juice and bring to the boil. Meanwhile, stir the cornflour into the kirsch, brandy, vodka or wine until smooth.
2. Reduce the heat slightly so that the wine is simmering gently, then pour the kirsch into the wine in a slow, steady drizzle, stirring constantly for 1–2 minutes until thickened slightly.
3. Now stir in the cheese, a handful at a time, stirring constantly and waiting until the cheese has melted before adding more. Once all of the cheese has been combined and the fondue is smooth and thick, scrape into a warmed fondue dish and place on a lit fondue base following manufacturer's instructions.
4. Serve the fondue with a selection of dippers.

TIPS If you don't have a proper fondue dish, transfer the saucepan directly to the table, placing it on a heatproof mat or board. You may need to reheat the pan gently from time to time as the fondue cools.

roast chicken with herbs & garlic

Cost
£££

Timing
⏱ ⏱ ⏱

Serves
4

what you need

- 8 garlic cloves, unpeeled
- 4 large thyme sprigs
- 3 large rosemary sprigs
- 1 organic or free-range chicken, about 1.75 kg (3½ lb)
- 1 tablespoon olive oil
- salt and pepper

what you do

1. Put the garlic cloves and half the herb sprigs in the body cavity of the chicken. Pat the chicken dry with kitchen paper and rub the oil all over the outside of the bird. Strip the leaves off the remaining herb sprigs and rub over the bird, with a little salt and pepper.
2. Place the chicken, breast-side up, in a roasting tin. Roast in a preheated oven, 220°C (425°F), Gas Mark 7, for 10 minutes. Turn the chicken over, breast-side down, reduce the oven temperature to 180°C (350°F), Gas Mark 4, and cook for a further 20 minutes. Finally, turn the chicken back to its original position and roast for another 25 minutes until the skin is crisp and golden. Check that the chicken is cooked by piercing the thigh with a knife. The juices should run clear, with no sign of pink. If not, cook for a further 10 minutes.
3. Transfer to a warmed serving plate and leave to rest for 5 minutes before serving with the pan juices.

for roast chicken with lemon & sage, cut a lemon in half, then cut 1 half into slices. Carefully lift the skin covering the breast meat and ease in the lemon slices. Put the other lemon half in the body cavity with 8 sage leaves, in place of the thyme and rosemary sprigs, and the garlic as opposite. Roast as opposite.

chicken & mushroom lasagne

what you need

- 8 chicken thighs
- 150 ml (¼ pint) dry white wine
- 300 ml (½ pint) chicken stock
- few stems thyme
- 2 tablespoons olive oil
- 2 onions, thinly sliced
- 2 garlic cloves, finely chopped
- 100 g (3½ oz) exotic mushrooms
- 125 g (4 oz) shiitake mushrooms, sliced
- 50 g (2 oz) butter
- 50 g (2 oz) plain flour
- 200 ml (7 fl oz) double cream
- 250 g (8 oz) pack of 6 fresh lasagne sheets
- 40 g (1½ oz) Parmesan cheese, freshly grated
- salt and pepper

what you do

1. Pack the chicken thighs into the base of a saucepan, add the wine, stock, thyme and a little seasoning. Bring to the boil, then cover and simmer for 45 minutes until tender.
2. Meanwhile, heat the oil in a frying pan, add the onions and fry for 5 minutes until just turning golden. Mix in the garlic and cook for 2–3 minutes, then stir in the mushrooms and fry for 2–3 minutes until golden.
3. Lift the chicken out of the pan, drain and set aside. Pour the stock into a measuring jug. Make up to 600 ml (1 pint) with water. Wash and dry the pan, then melt the butter in it. Stir in the flour, then gradually whisk in the stock and bring to the boil, stirring until thickened and smooth. Stir in the cream and adjust the seasoning, if needed.
4. Soak the lasagne sheets in boiling water for 5 minutes. Cut the skin and bones from the chicken and dice the meat. Drain the lasagne.
5. Pour a thin layer of sauce into the base of a 20 x 28 x 5 cm (8 x 11 x 2 inch) ovenproof dish or roasting tin, then cover with 2 sheets of lasagne. Spoon over half the mushroom mixture and half the chicken, then cover with a thin layer of sauce. Repeat the layers, then cover with the remaining lasagne and sauce. Sprinkle with the Parmesan.
6. Cook in a preheated oven, 190°C (375°F), Gas Mark 5, for 40 minutes until piping hot and the top is golden.

asian 5-spice glazed chicken

1. Toss the onion wedges in 1 tablespoon of the oil in a large roasting tin. Slash each chicken joint 2-3 times with a knife, then add to the roasting tin with the plums.

2. Warm the redcurrant jelly, vinegar, soy sauce and 5-spice in a small saucepan until the jelly has melted, then brush liberally over the chicken, reserving about one-third for later. Pour the measurement water into the base of the tin, avoiding the chicken, so that the glaze will not burn on the bottom of the tin.

3. Roast, uncovered in a preheated oven, 190°C (375°F), Gas Mark 5, for 40-45 minutes, brushing with the remaining glaze once during cooking. Test the chicken is done (see page 9).

4. Heat the remaining oil in a frying pan and add the pak choi. Fry for 2-3 minutes until tender and then add to the roasting tin just before serving.

what you need

- 2 red onions, cut into wedges
- 2 tablespoon sunflower oil
- 4 chicken thighs
- 4 chicken drumsticks
- 4 red plums, halved, stoned
- 3 tablespoons redcurrant jelly
- 1 tablespoon red wine vinegar
- 2 tablespoons dark soy sauce
- ½ teaspoon 5-spice powder
- 150 ml (¼ pint) water
- 100 g (3½ oz) pak choi

Cost
££

Timing

Serves
4

thai-style crab cakes with salsa

what you need

- 625 g (1¼ lb) fresh white crabmeat
- 400 g (13 oz) floury potatoes, cooked and mashed
- 2.5 cm (1 inch) piece of fresh root ginger, peeled and finely grated
- grated rind of 1 lime
- 1 red chilli, deseeded and finely chopped
- 1 tablespoon mayonnaise
- 5 tablespoons vegetable oil, for shallow-frying

black-eyed bean salsa
- 400 g (13 oz) can black-eyed beans, drained
- 1 red pepper, cored, deseeded and finely diced
- 300 g (10 oz) can sweetcorn, drained
- 3 tablespoons lime juice
- 2 tablespoons olive oil
- 2 tablespoons chopped coriander
- salt and pepper

what you do

1. Mix together the crab, potatoes, ginger, lime rind, chilli and mayonnaise. Season the mixture well with salt and pepper. Divide the mixture into 12 portions and shape into cakes with your hands.
2. Heat the vegetable oil in a frying pan and fry the crab cakes for 3–4 minutes on each side until they are golden brown.
3. Make the salsa by mixing together the beans, red pepper and sweetcorn. Squeeze over the lime juice and stir in the olive oil. Season with salt and pepper. Finally, mix in the chopped coriander.

spaghetti with seafood & fennel

Cost £££   **Timing** ⏱   **Serves** 4

what you need

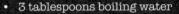

- 3 tablespoons boiling water
- ½ teaspoon saffron threads
- 15 g (1½ oz) butter
- 1 fennel bulb, sliced
- 50 ml (2 fl oz) dry white wine
- 450 g (14½ oz) mussels, debearded and cleaned
- 150 g (5 oz) crème fraîche
- 1 tablespoon olive oil
- 300 g (10 oz) monkfish fillet, boned and cut into 1.5 cm (¾ inch) thick slices
- 400 g (13 oz) spaghetti
- salt and pepper
- chopped tarragon leaves, to garnish

Pour the measurement water over the saffron in a heatproof bowl and leave to infuse.

Heat the butter in a large saucepan, add the fennel and cook over a medium heat for 5 minutes until softened. Pour over the wine and saffron with the soaking liquid and add the mussels. Cover with a lid and cook for 5 minutes until the mussels have opened. Discard any that remain closed. Stir through the crème fraîche and season.

Meanwhile, heat the oil in a nonstick frying pan, add the monkfish and cook over a high heat for 3 minutes on each side or until just cooked through. Carefully stir the monkfish into the mussel sauce.

While the mussel sauce is cooking, cook the pasta in a large saucepan of lightly salted boiling water according to the pack instructions until al dente. Drain, reserving a little of the cooking water. Stir through the mussel sauce, adding a little cooking water if needed, and season. Spoon into bowls and serve sprinkled with the tarragon.

salmon, prawn & spinach pie

what you do

what you need

- 675 g (1 lb 6 oz) puff pastry
- plain flour, for dusting
- 25 g (1 oz) butter
- 2 shallots, finely chopped
- grated rind of 1 lemon
- 2 tablespoons plain flour
- 300 ml (½ pint) single cream
- ½ teaspoon grated nutmeg
- 250 g (8 oz) frozen leaf spinach, thawed
- 500 g (1 lb) salmon fillet, pin-boned, skinned and cut into cubes
- 250 g (8 oz) raw peeled prawns
- 1 tablespoon chopped tarragon
- 1 egg, beaten
- salt and pepper

1. Roll out half the pastry on a lightly floured work surface to form a 25 x 35 cm (10 x 14 inch) rectangle. Repeat with the remaining pastry. Cover with clean tea towels and leave to rest.
2. Melt the butter in a saucepan and gently fry the shallots and lemon rind for 3 minutes. Stir in the flour and cook for 30 seconds. Remove from the heat, stir in the cream and then heat gently, stirring continuously, for 2 minutes until thickened. Remove from the heat and season with the nutmeg, salt and pepper. Cover with clingfilm and leave to cool.
3. Drain the spinach well and season with a little salt and pepper. Lay 1 piece of pastry on a large baking sheet lined with baking paper and spread the spinach over the top, leaving a 2.5 cm (1 inch) border at each end and a 5 cm (2 inch) border down each side. Stir the salmon, prawns and tarragon into the cooled cream mixture and spoon over the spinach. Brush the edges of the pastry with water and top with the other piece of pastry, pressing the edges together firmly.
4. Trim the pastry to neaten and then press the edges firmly together to seal. Brush with the beaten egg and pierce the top.
5. Bake on a pre-heated baking sheet in a preheated oven, 220°C (425°F), Gas Mark 7, for 20 minutes, then reduce the temperature to 190°C (375°F), Gas Mark 5, and bake for a further 15 minutes until the pastry is risen and golden.

sugar & spice salmon

Cost ££ **Timing** 🕐 **Serves** 4

what you need

- 4 salmon fillets, about 200 g (7 oz) each
- 3 tablespoons light muscovado sugar
- 2 garlic cloves, crushed
- 1 teaspoon cumin seeds, crushed
- 1 teaspoon smoked or sweet paprika
- 1 tablespoon white wine vinegar
- 3 tablespoons groundnut oil
- salt and pepper
- ½ teaspoon cumin seeds, crushed
- 2 courgettes, cut into thin ribbons
- lemon or lime slices, to serve

what you do

1. Put the salmon fillets in a lightly oiled roasting tin. Mix the sugar, garlic, cumin seeds, paprika, vinegar and a little salt in a bowl, then spread the mixture all over the fish so that it is thinly coated. Drizzle with 1 tablespoon of oil.
2. Bake in a preheated oven, 220°C (425°F), Gas Mark 7, for 10 minutes or until the fish is cooked through (see page 9).
3. Heat the remaining oil in a large frying pan, add the cumin seeds and fry for 10 seconds. Add the courgette ribbons, season with salt and pepper and stir-fry for 2-3 minutes until just softened.
4. Serve the salmon garnished with lemon or lime wedges.

greek lamb & tzatziki toasts

Cost
£££

Timing
◗ ◗ ◗

Serves
4

what you need

- 750 g (1½ lb) lamb chump chops
- 2 teaspoons dried oregano
- 3 garlic cloves, crushed
- 4 tablespoons olive oil
- 1 medium aubergine, about 300 g (10 oz), diced
- 2 red onions, sliced
- 200 ml (7 fl oz) white or red wine
- 400 g (13 oz) can chopped tomatoes
- 2 tablespoons clear honey
- 8 kalamata olives
- 8 thin slices French stick
- 200 g (7 oz) ready-made tzatziki
- salt and pepper

what you do

1. Cut the lamb into large pieces, discarding any excess fat. Mix the oregano with the garlic and a little seasoning and rub into the lamb.
2. Heat half the oil in a large saucepan or frying pan and fry the lamb in batches until browned. Drain to a plate.
3. Add the aubergine to the pan with the onions and remaining oil and cook very gently, stirring frequently, for about 10 minutes until softened and lightly browned. Return the meat to the pan with the wine, tomatoes, honey, olives and seasoning. Cover with a lid and cook on the lowest setting for about 1¼ hours or until the lamb is very tender.
4. Lightly toast the bread and spoon the tzatziki on top.
5. Check the stew for seasoning and turn into bowls. Serve with the toasts on the side.

meatballs with tomato sauce

Cost ££

Timing ●●●

Serves 4

what you need

- 500 g (1 lb) lean minced beef
- 3 garlic cloves, crushed
- 2 small onions, finely chopped
- 25 g (1 oz) breadcrumbs
- 40 g (1½ oz) freshly grated Parmesan cheese
- 6 tablespoons olive oil
- 100 ml (3½ fl oz) red wine
- 2 x 400 g (13 oz) cans chopped tomatoes
- 1 teaspoon caster sugar
- 3 tablespoons sun-dried tomato paste
- 75 g (3 oz) pitted Italian black olives, roughly chopped
- 4 tablespoons roughly chopped oregano
- 125 g (4 oz) mozzarella cheese, thinly sliced
- salt and pepper
- warmed, crusty bread, to serve

what you do

1. Put the beef in a bowl with half the crushed garlic and half the onion, the breadcrumbs and 25 g (1 oz) of the Parmesan. Season and use your hands to thoroughly blend the ingredients together. Shape into small balls, about 2.5 cm (1 inch) in diameter.
2. Heat half the oil in a large frying pan and fry the meatballs, shaking the pan frequently, for about 10 minutes until browned. Drain.
3. Add the remaining oil and onion to the pan and fry until softened. Add the wine and let the mixture bubble until the wine has almost evaporated. Stir in the remaining garlic, the tomatoes, sugar, tomato paste and a little seasoning. Bring to the boil and let the mixture bubble until slightly thickened.
4. Stir in the olives, all but 1 tablespoon of the oregano and the meatballs. Cook gently for a further 5 minutes.
5. Arrange the mozzarella slices over the top and scatter with the remaining oregano and Parmesan. Season with pepper and cook under the grill until the cheese starts to melt. Serve in bowls with warmed, crusty bread.

Berry muffins

Eton mess

Choc chip cookies

Sweet Stuff

raspberry ripple meringues

Cost
£

Timing
◗ ◗ ◗

Makes
12

what you need

- 40 g (1½ oz) fresh raspberries, plus extra to serve (optional)
- 2 tablespoons raspberry jam
- 4 egg whites
- 200 g (7 oz) caster sugar

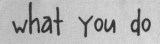

what you do

1. Put the raspberries in a bowl and mash with a fork until broken up and turning juicy. Add the jam and mash together to make a purée. Tip into a sieve resting over a small bowl and press the purée with the back of a spoon to extract as much juice as possible.
2. Whisk the egg whites in a large clean bowl with a hand-held electric whisk until peaking. Whisk in a tablespoonful of the sugar and continue to whisk for about 15 seconds. Gradually add the remaining sugar, a spoonful at a time, until thick and glossy.
3. Drizzle over the raspberry purée and lightly stir in using a spatula or large metal spoon, scooping up the meringue from the base of the bowl so that the mixture is streaked with the purée. Do not to over-mix.
4. Drop large spoonfuls of the mixture, each about the size of a small orange, on to a large baking sheet lined with baking parchment, then swirl with the back of a teaspoon. Bake in a preheated oven, 120°C (250°F), Gas Mark ½, for about 1¼ hours or until the meringues are crisp and come away easily from the paper. Leave to cool on the paper. Serve with extra raspberries, if liked.

chocolate & marshmallow torte

Cost
££

Timing

Serves
8

what you need

- 200 g (7 oz) plain dark chocolate, broken into pieces
- 100 g (3½ oz) unsalted butter
- 5 eggs, separated
- 175 g (6 oz) caster sugar
- 2 tablespoons plain flour, sifted
- ½ teaspoon ground cinnamon
- 2 tablespoons warm water
- 300 ml (½ pint) double cream
- 125 g (4 oz) mini pink and white marshmallows

for mixed nut torte, fold in 100 g (3½ oz) mixed pistachios, hazelnuts and almonds, roughly chopped, after the flour and cinnamon. Serve with 4 tablespoons toasted flaked almonds instead of the marshmallows.

what you do

1. Put the chocolate and butter in a bowl set over a saucepan of gently simmering water and leave to melt.
2. Whisk the egg whites in a large bowl until stiff, moist-looking peaks are formed, then gradually whisk in half the sugar, a teaspoonful at a time, until thick and glossy. Using the still dirty whisk, beat the egg yolks and remaining sugar in a third bowl until very thick.
3. Mix the warm chocolate and butter mixture gradually into the egg yolks. Stir in the flour and cinnamon, then loosen the mixture with the measurement warm water. Gently fold in a spoonful of the meringue, then fold in the remainder.
4. Pour the mixture into a greased and base-lined 23 cm (9 inch) springform tin. Bake in a preheated oven, 180°C (350°F), Gas Mark 4, for 25–30 minutes until well risen and the top is crusty and the centre only just set. Leave to cool for 2 hours in the tin.
5. Remove the torte from the tin, discarding the lining paper. Cut into wedges. Softly whip the cream, then top wedges of torte with spoonfuls of cream and a sprinkling of marshmallows.

creamy vanilla rice pudding

Cost £

Timing ⏲ ⏲

Serves 4

what you do

1. Place all the ingredients in a saucepan and bring to the boil. Reduce the heat and simmer gently for 25–28 minutes, stirring frequently and adding more milk if necessary, until the rice is creamy and just tender.
2. Remove the vanilla pod, if using, spoon the rice pudding into bowls and serve immediately.

what you need

- 125 g (4 oz) pudding rice
- about 750 ml (1¼ pints) whole milk
- 50 g (2 oz) caster sugar
- 1 teaspoon vanilla extract or 1 vanilla pod, split
- 25 g (1 oz) butter

lovely leftovers

Any leftover rice pudding is delicious served cold with a handful of summer berries or with a dollop of homemade blueberry jam (see page 138), or simply dusted with cinnamon.

blackberry crumble

Cost
£

Timing

Serves
4

what you need

- 750 g (1½ lb) blackberries
- 2 oranges, segmented
- zest and juice of 1 orange
- 200 g (7 oz) butter
- 200 g (7 oz) plain flour
- 100 g (3½ oz) soft brown sugar
- cream, ice cream or custard, to serve (optional)

what you do

1. Mix the blackberries, orange segments and the orange zest and juice together in a bowl.
2. In a separate bowl rub together the butter and flour with your fingertips until it resembles breadcrumbs and then stir in the sugar.
3. Tip the blackberry mixture into a large ovenproof dish and scatter over the crumble mixture to cover.
4. Bake in a preheated oven, 220°C (425°F), Gas Mark 7, for 20–25 minutes until golden. Remove from the oven and serve warm with cream, ice cream or custard, if liked.

choco bread & butter pudding

what you need

- 4 chocolate croissants
- 50 g (2 oz) unsalted butter
- 50 g (2 oz) caster sugar
- ¼ teaspoon ground mixed spice
- 300 ml (½ pint) milk
- 4 eggs
- 1 teaspoon vanilla essence
- icing sugar, to decorate
- single cream, to serve

for fruited bread & butter pudding,

lightly butter 8 slices of white bread, cut into triangles and arrange in slightly overlapping layers in the dish, sprinkling with 75 g (3 oz) luxury dried fruit between the layers. Add the sugar as above, but omit the mixed spice. Mix the eggs, milk and vanilla, pour over the bread, then continue as above.

what you do

Grease a 1.2 litre (2 pint) shallow, round, ovenproof pie dish. Slice the croissants thickly and spread the butter over one side of each cut face of croissant. Stand the croissant slices upright and close together in the dish to completely fill it.

Mix the sugar and spice together, then spoon over the croissants and between the gaps. Stand the dish in a large roasting tin.

Beat the milk, eggs and vanilla essence together, then strain into the dish. Leave to stand for 15 minutes.

Pour hot water from the tap into the roasting tin to come halfway up the sides of the pie dish. Bake in a preheated oven, 180°C (350°F), Gas Mark 4, for about 25 minutes until the pudding is golden and the custard just set.

Lift the dish out of the roasting tin, dust with sifted icing sugar and serve the pudding warm with a little single cream.

blueberry & orange eton mess

Cost ££

Timing ⏱

Serves 4

what you need

- 250 ml (8 fl oz) fresh chilled custard
- 200 g (7 oz) blueberry yogurt
- 1 teaspoon finely grated orange rind
- 1 teaspoon vanilla bean paste or extract
- 150 g (5 oz) blueberries
- 4 ready-made meringues nests, about 50 g (2 oz) total weight

what you do

1. Put the custard, yogurt, orange rind and vanilla bean paste or extract in a bowl and stir until well combined.
2. Put two-thirds of the blueberries in 4 tall glasses. Spoon over the blueberry yogurt mixture, then top each glass with a lightly crushed meringue. Sprinkle over the remaining blueberries and serve immediately.

easy peasy chocolate sauce

Cost £

Timing 🕐

Serves 4

what you need

- 175 g (6 oz) evaporated milk
- 100 g (3½ oz) plain dark chocolate, broken into pieces

for easy minty choc sauce,

use 100 g (31/2 oz) plain dark mint chocolate instead of plain dark chocolate. Finely chop 6 fresh mint leaves and add to the mint chocolate and evaporated milk mixture. Heat gently, stirring until the chocolate is melted.

what you do

1. Tip the evaporated milk into a pan, add the chocolate and heat gently for 2-3 minutes, stirring until the chocolate is melted.
2. Serve immediately with the dessert of your choice. This sauce goes particularly well with ice cream.

lime & passion fruit crunch tart

Cost
££

Timing
◐ ◐

Serves
6-8

what you need

- 100 g (3½ oz) unsalted butter
- 2 tablespoons golden syrup
- 250 g (8 oz) digestive biscuits, crushed
- 300 ml (½ pint) double cream
- grated rind and juice of 3 limes

- 400 g (13 oz) can full-fat condensed milk

to decorate
- 3 passion fruit, halved
- 150 g (5 oz) blueberries

what you do

1. Heat the butter and golden syrup in a saucepan, stir in the biscuit crumbs and mix well. Tip into a greased 23 cm (9 inch) springform tin, and press over the base of the tin with the end of a rolling pin. Chill while making the filling.
2. Whip the cream in a large bowl until it forms soft swirls. Add the lime rind and condensed milk and gently fold together, then gradually mix in the lime juice. Pour over the biscuit base and freeze for 4 hours or overnight.
3. Loosen the edge of the tart from the tin with a round-bladed knife, remove the sides, then slide off the base on to a serving plate. Spoon the seeds from the passion fruit over the top, then scatter with the blueberries. Allow to soften for 30 minutes before cutting into slices.

chunky monkeys

Cost ££   **Timing**   **Makes** 12

what you need

- 200 g (7 oz) plain flour
- 1 teaspoon bicarbonate of soda
- 125 g (4 oz) caster sugar
- 125 g (4 oz) butter, chilled and diced
- 1 egg
- 1 tablespoon milk
- 150 g (5 oz) white chocolate, roughly chopped
- 75 g (3 oz) natural glacé cherries, roughly chopped

what you do

1. Mix together the flour, bicarbonate of soda and sugar in a bowl. Add the butter and rub in with the fingertips until the mixture resembles breadcrumbs.
2. Beat together the egg and milk in a separate bowl. Add the chopped chocolate and glacé cherries, then mix into the flour mixture and stir well until smooth.
3. Drop heaped tablespoonfuls of the mixture, well spaced apart, on to a greased baking sheet and bake in a preheated oven, 180°C (350°F), Gas Mark 4, for 10–12 minutes until lightly golden. Leave to harden on the sheet for 2 minutes, then transfer to a wire rack to cool.

for double chocolate chunky monkeys,

make the biscuits as above, replacing 15 g (1/2 oz) of the flour with 15 g (1/2 oz) cocoa powder and the cherries with 75 g (3 oz) toasted blanched hazelnuts, roughly chopped.

peanut butter cookies

Cost
££

Timing

Makes
18–20

what you need

- 75 g (3 oz) crunchy peanut butter
- 100 g (3½ oz) golden caster sugar
- 50 g (2 oz) slightly salted butter, softened
- 1 egg, beaten
- 100 g (3½ oz) self-raising flour
- 40 g (1½ oz) salted peanuts, chopped

what you do

1. Beat together the peanut butter, sugar and butter in a bowl until well combined. Add the egg and flour and mix to a paste.
2. Roll teaspoonfuls of the mixture into small walnut-sized balls, then place slightly apart on a large greased baking sheet and flatten with a fork. Scatter the chopped peanuts over the cookies.
3. Bake in a preheated oven, 180°C (350°F), Gas Mark 4, for around 18–20 minutes until risen and deep golden. Transfer to a wire rack to cool.

TIPS These super-easy cookies make a fab handheld dessert sandwiched either side of a dollop of your favourite ice cream.

choc chip cookies

Cost
££

Timing
⏱ ⏱

Makes
16

what you do

what you need

- 125 g (4 oz) unsalted butter, softened
- 175 g (6 oz) soft light brown sugar
- 1 teaspoon vanilla extract
- 1 egg, lightly beaten
- 1 tablespoon milk
- 200 g (7 oz) plain flour
- 1 teaspoon baking powder
- 250 g (8 oz) plain chocolate chips

1. Beat together the butter and sugar in a large bowl until pale and fluffy. Add the vanilla, then gradually beat in the egg, beating well after each addition. Stir in the milk. Sift in the flour and baking powder, then fold in. Stir in the plain chocolate chips.

2. Drop level tablespoonfuls of the mixture, about 3.5 cm (1½ inches) apart, on a large baking sheet lined with baking parchment; lightly press with a floured fork. Bake in a preheated oven, 180°C (350°F), Gas Mark 4, for 15 minutes or until lightly golden. Transfer to a wire rack to cool.

banoffee pie

Cost ££

Timing

Serves 4

what you need

- 200 g (7 oz) amaretti biscuits, lightly crushed
- 100 g (3½ oz) unsalted butter, melted
- 397 g (13 oz) can caramel
- 3 bananas, sliced
- 200 ml (7 fl oz) double cream
- 30 g (1¼ oz) plain dark chocolate, grated

what you do

1. Place the crushed amaretti biscuits in a bowl, pour over the melted butter and mix well.
2. Pour the buttered crumbs into a 20 cm (8 inch) loose-bottomed flan tin and press them into the base and sides. Chill for 10 minutes.
3. Spread the caramel over the biscuit base, then top with the sliced bananas.
4. Whip the cream to soft peaks and spread over the bananas. Scatter the grated chocolate over the top.

banana & raisin flapjacks

Cost £

Timing 🕐

Makes 12

what you do

what you need

- 150 g (5 oz) butter
- 150 ml (¼ pint) maple syrup
- 125 g (4 oz) raisins
- 2 large bananas, well mashed
- 375 g (12 oz) porridge oats

1. Place the butter in a medium saucepan with the maple syrup and melt over a gentle heat. Stir in the raisins. Remove from the heat and add the bananas, stirring well. Add the oats and stir well until all the oats have been coated.

2. Spoon the mixture into a 28 x 18 cm (11 x 7 inch) nonstick roasting tin and level the surface using a potato masher for ease. Bake in a preheated oven, 190°C (375°F), Gas Mark 5, for 10 minutes until the top is just beginning to turn a pale golden. The mixture will still seem somewhat soft.

3. Allow to cool for 10 minutes in the tin before cutting into 12 squares. Remove from the tin and allow to cool completely.

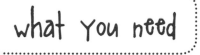

rum & raisin chocolate brownies

Cost
££

Timing

Makes
20

what you need

- 3 tablespoons white or dark rum
- 100 g (3½ oz) raisins
- 250 g (8 oz) plain dark chocolate, broken into pieces
- 250 g (8 oz) butter
- 4 eggs
- 200 g (7 oz) caster sugar
- 75 g (3 oz) self-raising flour
- 1 teaspoon baking powder
- 100 g (3½ oz) white or milk chocolate

For triple choc brownies, omit the rum and raisins and instead sprinkle 100 g (3½ oz) finely chopped milk chocolate and 100 g (3½ oz) finely chopped white chocolate over the mixture just before baking. Bake as above then omit the melted chocolate topping.

Warm the rum, add the raisins and leave to soak for 2 hours or overnight. Heat the dark chocolate and butter gently in a saucepan until both have melted. Meanwhile, whisk the eggs and sugar together in a bowl, using an electric whisk, until very thick and the whisk leaves a trail when lifted above the mixture.

Fold the warm chocolate and butter into the whisked eggs and sugar. Sift the flour and baking powder over the top then fold in. Pour the mixture into an 18 x 28 cm (7 x 11 inch) roasting tin lined with nonstick baking paper, and ease into the corners. Spoon the rum-soaked raisins over the top. Bake in a preheated oven, 180°C (350°F), Gas Mark 4, for around 25–30 minutes until well risen, the top is crusty and cracked and the centre still slightly soft. Leave to cool and harden in the tin.

Lift out of the tin using the lining paper. Melt the white or milk chocolate in a heatproof bowl set over a saucepan of gently simmering water then drizzle over the top of the brownies. Leave to harden then cut into 20 pieces. Peel off the paper and store in an airtight tin for up to 3 days.

rocky road slices

what you need

- 225 g (7½ oz) butter
- 3 tablespoons golden syrup
- 50 g (2 oz) cocoa powder
- 125 g (4 oz) digestive biscuits, roughly crushed
- 200 g (7 oz) marshmallows, each cut into 4
- 75 g (3 oz) Maltesers, roughly crushed
- 200 g (7 oz) milk chocolate
- 200 g (7 oz) plain dark chocolate
- 4 tablespoons chocolate sprinkles

what you do

1. Melt the butter with the golden syrup and cocoa powder in a bowl over a pan of simmering water. Stir in the biscuits, marshmallows and Maltesers.
2. Grease a 25 x 18 cm (10 x 7 inch) tin. Pour the biscuit mixture into the prepared tin and chill for 15 minutes.
3. Melt the milk and plain chocolate together in a bowl over a pan of simmering water. Remove from the heat. Pour the chocolate over the chilled mixture and scatter with chocolate sprinkles.
4. Chill for 20 minutes, then cut into slices or squares.

choc cornflake bars

Cost
£

Timing
⏱

Makes
12

what you need

- 200 g (7 oz) milk chocolate, broken into pieces
- 2 tablespoons golden syrup
- 50 g (2 oz) butter
- 125 g (4 oz) cornflakes

what you do

1. Melt the chocolate with the golden syrup and butter in a bowl over a pan of simmering water.
2. Stir in the cornflakes and mix well together.
3. Grease a 28 x 18 cm (11 x 7 inch) tin. Turn the mixture into the tin, chill until set, then cut into 12 bars.

for muesli & apricot crunch cakes,
replace the cornflakes with 125 g (4 oz) muesli and 50 g (2 oz) chopped dried apricots. Combine with the chocolate mixture, spoon into 12 paper cake cases and chill until set.

for homemade blueberry jam, put 500 g (1 lb)
fresh blueberries, 4 tablespoons lemon juice and 2 tablespoons water in a large saucepan and cook gently for about 8-10 minutes until the berries are soft. Stir in 450 g (14 1/2 oz) preserving or granulated sugar and heat gently until the sugar dissolves. Bring to the boil and boil for 10-15 minutes until setting point is reached. Ladle into sterilized jars, cover and label.

blueberry bakewell

Cost ££

Timing

Serves 18

- 350 g (11½ oz) ready-made sweet shortcrust pastry
- 6 tablespoons blueberry jam (see opposite for homemade)
- 125 g (4 oz) slightly salted butter, softened
- 125 g (4 oz) caster sugar

- 2 eggs
- 125 g (4 oz) self-raising flour
- ½ teaspoon baking powder
- 1 teaspoon almond extract
- 100 g (3½ oz) ground almonds
- 4 tablespoons flaked almonds
- 75 g (3 oz) icing sugar, sifted

what you do

1. Roll out the pastry on a lightly floured surface and use to line a greased 28 x 18 cm (11 x 7 inch) shallow baking tin. Line the pastry case with baking parchment and baking beans (or dried beans). Bake in a preheated oven, 200°C (400°F), Gas Mark 4, for 15 minutes. Remove the paper and beans and bake for a further 5 minutes. Reduce the oven temperature to 180°C (350°F), Gas Mark 4.
2. Spread the base of the pastry with the jam. Beat together the butter, caster sugar, eggs, flour, baking powder and almond extract in a bowl until smooth and creamy. Beat in the ground almonds. Spoon the mixture over the jam and spread gently in an even layer.
3. Scatter with the flaked almonds and bake for about 40 minutes until risen and just firm to the touch. Leave to cool in the tin.
4. Beat the icing sugar with a dash of water in a bowl to give the consistency of thin cream. Spread in a thin layer over the cake. Allow to set, then cut into squares or fingers.

banana, date & walnut loaf

Cost
££

Timing
● ● ●

Serves
10

what you need

- 400 g (13 oz) bananas, weighed with skins on
- 1 tablespoon lemon juice
- 300 g (10 oz) self-raising flour
- 1 teaspoon baking powder
- 125 g (4 oz) caster sugar
- 125 g (4 oz) butter, melted
- 2 eggs, beaten
- 175 g (6 oz) ready-chopped dried dates
- 50 g (2 oz) walnut pieces
- walnut halves and banana chips, to decorate (optional)

TIPS This loaf will keep for up to 5 days in an airtight container — if it lasts that long!

what you do

1. Peel then mash the bananas with the lemon juice.
2. Put the flour, baking powder and sugar in a mixing bowl. Add the mashed bananas, melted butter and eggs and mix together. Stir in the dates and walnut pieces then spoon into a greased 1 kg (2 lb) loaf tin, its base and 2 long sides also lined with oiled greaseproof paper. Spread the surface level and decorate the top with walnut halves and banana chips, if using.
3. Bake in the centre of a preheated oven, 160°C (325°F), Gas Mark 3, for 1 hour 10 minutes–1¼ hours until well risen, the top has cracked and a skewer inserted into the centre comes out clean. Leave to cool for 10 minutes then loosen the edges, turn out on to a wire rack and peel off the lining paper. Leave to cool completely.

sultana & ginger cupcakes

what you need

- 50 g (2 oz) piece of fresh root ginger
- 125 g (4 oz) lightly salted butter, softened
- 125 g (4 oz) caster sugar
- 2 eggs
- 150 g (5 oz) self-raising flour
- ½ teaspoon baking powder
- ½ teaspoon vanilla extract
- 50 g (2 oz) sultanas
- 200 g (7 oz) icing sugar
- several pieces of crystallized ginger, very thinly sliced, to decorate

what you do

1. Line a 12-section muffin tray with paper cake cases.
2. Peel and finely grate the ginger, working over a plate to catch the juice. Put the butter, caster sugar, eggs, flour, baking powder and vanilla extract in a bowl. Add the grated ginger, reserving the juice for the icing. Beat with a hand-held electric whisk for about a minute until light and creamy.
3. Stir in the sultanas and then divide the cake mixture between the paper cases.
4. Bake in a preheated oven, 180°C (350°F), Gas Mark 4, for 20 minutes or until risen and just firm to the touch. Transfer to a wire rack to cool.
5. Beat the icing sugar in a bowl with the ginger juice, making up with enough water to create an icing that just holds its shape. Spread over the tops of the cakes with a small palette knife. Decorate with the crystallized ginger slices.

double berry muffins

what you do

1. Line a 12-section muffin tray with paper muffin cases. Put the flour, baking powder and sugar in a bowl and stir together using a fork.
2. Melt the butter in a small saucepan over a gentle heat and pour into the dry ingredients. Add the eggs, oil, vanilla extract and yogurt and stir together until only just combined. Stir in the fresh berries. Divide the muffin mixture between the paper cases.
3. Bake in a preheated oven, 200°C (400°F), Gas Mark 6, for 15 minutes or until the muffins are well risen and the tops have cracked and turned golden brown.
4. Loosen the edges of the paper cases with a round-bladed knife to serve warm or transfer to a wire rack to cool.

what you need

- 300 g (10 oz) plain flour
- 3 teaspoons baking powder
- 125 g (4 oz) caster sugar
- 50 g (2 oz) lightly salted butter
- 3 eggs
- 4 tablespoons sunflower oil
- 1½ teaspoons vanilla extract
- 150 g (5 oz) natural yogurt
- 100 g (3½ oz) fresh blueberries
- 100 g (3½ oz) fresh raspberries

Margarita

Mojito

Rattlesnake

The Bar is Open

strawberry daiquiri

Cost
£££

Makes
1

what you need

1. Muddle the strawberries, syrup and mint leaves in the bottom of a cocktail shaker.
2. Add the rum and lime juice, shake with ice and double-strain into a chilled martini glass. Decorate with a strawberry slice and a sprig of mint.

- 3 strawberries, hulled
- dash of strawberry syrup
- 6 mint leaves, plus a sprig to decorate
- 2 measures golden rum
- 2 measures lime juice
- strawberry slice, to decorate

TIPS Muddling is a technique to bring out the flavours in fruit and herbs. Use the end of wooden spoon to press and mash the ingredients against the side of a cocktail shaker or glass.

sea breeze

Cost
£££

Makes
2

what you need

- ice cubes
- 2 measures vodka
- 4 measures cranberry juice
- 2 measures grapefruit juice
- lime wedges, to decorate

what you do

1. Fill 2 tall glasses with ice cubes, pour over the vodka, cranberry juice and grapefruit juice and stir well.
2. Decorate with lime wedges and serve.

mojito

Cost
£££

Makes
2

what you need

- 16 mint leaves, plus sprigs to decorate
- 1 lime, cut into wedges
- 4 teaspoons cane sugar
- crushed ice
- 5 measures white rum
- soda water, to top up

what you do

1. Muddle the mint leaves, lime and sugar in the bottom of 2 tall glasses and fill with crushed ice.
2. Add the rum, stir and top up with soda water.
3. Decorate with mint sprigs and serve.

for a Limon Mojito,
muddle the quarters of 2 limes with 4 teaspoons of soft brown sugar and 16 mint leaves in the bottom of 2 tall glasses, then add 4 measures of Limon Bacardi rum instead of the 5 measures of white rum. Stir and top up with soda water.

cuba libre

Cost
£££

Makes
2

what you need

- ice cubes
- 4 measures golden rum, such as Havana Club 3-year-old
- juice of 1 lime
- cola, to top up
- lime wedges

what you do

Fill 2 tall glasses with ice cubes. Pour over the rum and lime juice and stir. Top up with cola, decorate with lime wedges and serve with straws.

TIPS Have a hunt around your local charity shops for some inexpensive fancy glasses – ideal for cocktail hour.

classic martini

what you need

- ice cubes
- 1 measure dry vermouth
- 6 measures gin
- stuffed green olives, to garnish

what you do

1. Put 10–12 ice cubes into a mixing glass.
2. Pour over the vermouth and gin and stir (never shake) vigorously and evenly without splashing. Strain into 2 chilled martini glasses, decorate each with a green olive and serve.

Cost
£££

Makes
2

pimm's cocktail

what you need

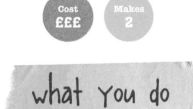

Cost
£££

Makes
2

- ice cubes
- 2 measures Pimm's No. 1
- 2 measures gin
- 4 measures lemonade
- 4 measures ginger ale

to decorate
- cucumber strips
- blueberries
- orange slices

what you do

1. Fill 2 tall glass with ice cubes.
2. Add the remaining ingredients, one by one in order, over the ice. Decorate with cucumber strips, blueberries and orange slices and serve.

margarita

Cost £££

Makes 2

what you need

- 2 lime wedges
- rock salt
- 4 measures Herrudura Reposado tequila
- 2 measures lime juice
- 2 measures Triple Sec
- ice cubes
- lime slices, to decorate

what you do

Rub the rim of each margarita glass with a lime wedge, then dip it into rock salt.

Pour the tequila, lime juice and Triple Sec into a cocktail shaker and add some ice cubes. Shake and strain into the salt-rimmed glasses. Decorate each glass with a slice of lime and serve.

rattlesnake

Cost £££

Makes 2

what you need

- ice cubes, plus extra to serve
- 3 measures whisky
- 2 teaspoons lemon juice
- 2 teaspoons sugar syrup
- 2 egg whites
- few drops Pernod
- lime wedges, to decorate

what you do

1. Put 8–10 ice cubes, the whisky, lemon juice, sugar syrup, egg whites and Pernod into a cocktail shaker and shake extremely well.
2. Strain into 2 glasses, add some more ice and serve with lime wedges.

for a kicker,

which is one of the simplest whisky-based cocktails, to serve one, mix 1 measure of whisky with 1 measure of Midori and serve chilled or with ice.

early night

Cost
£££

Makes
2

what you need

- 2 tablespoons lemon juice
- 2 measures clear honey
- 2 measures whisky
- 4 measures boiling water
- 2 measures ginger wine
- lemon slices, to decorate

what you do

1. Put the lemon juice and honey into 2 heatproof glasses and stir well. Add the whisky and continue stirring.
2. Stir in the boiling water, then add the ginger wine.
3. Decorate each glass with lemon slices. Serve at once and drink while still hot.

TIPS This is a traditional cure-all for colds, coughs and the winter blues. You can make a comforting non-alcoholic version by leaving out the whisky and ginger wine and spicing things up with ground ginger and cinnamon instead.

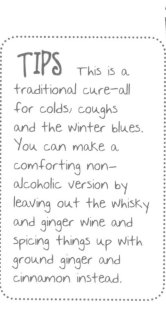

sangria

what you need

- ice cubes
- 2 bottles light Spanish red wine, chilled
- 5 measures brandy
- orange, lemon and apple wedges
- cinnamon sticks
- about 450 ml (¾ pint) chilled lemonade, to top up
- lemon slices, to decorate

what you do

1. Put some ice cubes into a very large jug. Add the wine, brandy, fruit wedges and one cinnamon stick and stir well.
2. Top up with lemonade when you are ready to serve, and stir. Serve in glasses decorated with lemon slices and cinnamon sticks.

Sausage & cheesy beans

Hot chocolate

Blueberry pancakes

Hangover Helpers

hangover express

Cost £

Timing 🕐

Serves 1

what you need

- 150 g (5 oz) broccoli, broken into florets
- 2 dessert apples, cored and quartered
- 150 g (5 oz) spinach
- ice cubes

what you do

1. Juice the broccoli, apples and spinach in a juicer or blender, alternating the spinach with the broccoli and apple so that the machine does not get clogged up with the leaves.
2. Mix with a couple of ice cubes before serving, to dilute slightly, as this juice is very sweet.

for broccoli lemon express, Juice the broccoli and dessert apples, then stir in 1 tablespoon fresh lemon juice. Serve with ice.

the rehydrator

what you need

- 1 orange
- 50 g (2 oz) cucumber
- 100 ml (3½ fl oz) cranberry juice
- ice cubes

what you do

1. Peel the orange, leaving on as much pith as possible. Using a juicer or blender, juice the orange and cucumber until smooth.
2. Mix the orange and cucumber juice with the cranberry juice, then pour into a tall glass over ice. Serve with cucumber stick stirrers.

for strawberry rehydrator, omit the cucumber and juice the orange with 250 g (8 oz) fresh strawberries. Mix with the cranberry juice and 1 teaspoon clear honey, blending or stirring until the honey is dissolved.

all-day breakfast wrap

what you need

- 1 tablespoon vegetable oil, plus extra for greasing
- 375 g (12 oz) pork sausagemeat
- 250 g (8 oz) mushrooms, sliced
- 2 large eggs
- 2 tomatoes, deseeded and diced
- 4 large soft flour tortillas
- salt and pepper
- brown sauce, barbecue sauce or tomato ketchup, to serve (optional)

what you do

1. Preheat the oven to 200°C (400°F), Gas Mark 6, and lightly grease a baking sheet. Divide the sausagemeat into 4 long, flat sausages. Place on the baking sheet and cook in the preheated oven for 15–18 minutes, turning once, until cooked through.
2. Meanwhile, heat the oil in a frying pan and cook the mushrooms for 4–5 minutes, until softened and golden. Transfer to a bowl and keep warm. Place the frying pan back over a medium heat.
3. Crack the eggs into a bowl and beat lightly. Stir in the chopped tomato, season with salt and pepper and pour into the hot frying pan. Stir gently until it starts to set, then cook for 1–2 minutes, until the base is golden and the omelette is just set. Slide on to a chopping board and slice thickly.
4. Place 1 baked sausage in the centre of each tortilla, then top with some mushrooms and strips of omelette. Roll tightly and cut in half diagonally. Serve hot with brown sauce, barbecue sauce or tomato ketchup, if liked.

cinnamon french toasts

Cost £

Timing

Serves 4

what you need

- 2 eggs, beaten
- 1 teaspoon vanilla extract
- 100 ml (3½ fl oz) milk
- 1 tablespoon caster sugar, plus extra for sprinkling
- ½ teaspoon ground cinnamon
- 4 thick slices of bread
- 25 g (1 oz) butter

what you do

1. Whisk together the eggs, vanilla extract, milk, sugar and cinnamon in a shallow dish. Place the slices of bread in the mixture, turning to coat both sides so that they absorb the liquid.
2. Heat the butter in a nonstick frying pan. Use a palette knife or a fish slice to remove the soaked bread from the dish and fry the slices for 2 minutes on each side until golden. Cut the toasts in half diagonally into triangles, sprinkle with a little caster sugar and serve.

for apple & raspberry sauce,

heat 25 g (1 oz) butter in a frying pan, add 6 cored, sliced eating apples and fry for 2–3 minutes. Sprinkle over 1 tablespoon soft light brown sugar, 1/2 teaspoon ground cinnamon and 125 g (4 oz) raspberries and cook gently for 1–2 minutes. Serve over the toasts.

boiled eggs with mustard soldiers

what you need

- 2 teaspoons wholegrain mustard, or to taste
- 50 g (2 oz) unsalted butter, softened
- 4 large eggs
- 4 thick slices of white bread
- pepper
- mustard and cress, to serve

what you do

1. Beat the mustard, butter and pepper together in a small bowl.
2. Cook the eggs in a saucepan of boiling water for 4–5 minutes until softly set. Meanwhile, toast the bread, then butter one side with the mustard butter and cut into fingers.
3. Serve the eggs with the mustard soldiers and some mustard and cress.

Cost
£

Timing

Serves
4

sausage & cheese baked beans

Cost
££

Timing
🕐

Serves
2

what you need

- 4 herby farmhouse sausages
- 1 tablespoon vegetable oil
- 1 garlic clove, crushed
- 1 teaspoon paprika (optional)
- 1 teaspoon onion powder or granules (optional)
- 400 g (13 oz) can haricot beans, rinsed and drained
- 350 g (11½ oz) passata or sieved tomatoes
- 1 teaspoon Worcestershire sauce
- 1 teaspoon dark brown sugar or black treacle
- 2-4 slices of your preferred bread
- butter, for spreading
- 100 g (3½ oz) Cheddar cheese, grated

TIPS The beans will improve in flavour stored in the fridge a day or two so you can double up the recipe and serve the rest on top of baked potatoes or with the toad in the hole on page 54.

what you do

Arrange the sausages on the rack of a foil-lined grill tray and slide the tray under a grill preheated to a medium setting. Grill the sausages for about 15 minutes, turning occasionally, until cooked through and golden. Remove and keep warm.

While the sausages are cooking, heat the oil in a saucepan and cook the garlic gently for 1 minute before adding the paprika, if using. Cook for a further minute, then add the onion powder or granules (if using), beans, passata or sieved tomatoes, Worcestershire sauce and sugar or treacle. Simmer gently for about 15 minutes until the beans are soft and the sauce has thickened slightly. Towards the end of the cooking time for the beans and sausages, toast and butter the slices of bread.

Slice the sausages thickly, then combine with the beans. According to preference, either stir the cheese into the mixture, then spoon it onto the slices of buttered toast, or spoon the beans-and-sausage mixture onto the slices of buttered toast and sprinkle over the grated Cheddar cheese.

luxury hot chocolate

Cost
££

Timing

Serves
4

what you need

- 100 g (3½ oz) good-quality plain dark chocolate, broken into small pieces
- 25 g (1 oz) caster sugar
- 750 ml (1¼ pints) milk
- a few drops of vanilla extract
- pinch of ground cinnamon
- mini marshmallows, to serve

what you do

1. Put the chocolate and sugar in a heavy-based saucepan. Pour in the milk, then add the vanilla extract and cinnamon.
2. Cover and gently heat, whisking once or twice, until the chocolate has melted. Continue heating until the mixture is steaming hot, but do not allow to boil.
3. Ladle the hot chocolate into 4 large cups or mugs and top with a few mini marshmallows. Serve immediately while steaming hot.

chocolate brioche sandwich

Cost
££

Timing
🕐

Serves
1

what you need

- 2 slices brioche
- 1 tablespoon chocolate spread
- 15 g (½ oz) butter
- 2 teaspoons golden granulated sugar

what you do

1. Spread 1 slice of brioche with chocolate spread, then top with the other slice.
2. Butter the outsides of the chocolate sandwich and sprinkle with the sugar.
3. Heat a griddle, frying pan or sandwich maker, and cook the chocolate brioche for 3 minutes, turning as needed.

for peanut butter & choc brioche sandwich,

spread 1 slice brioche with 1 tablespoon chocolate spread and the other slice with 1 tablespoon peanut butter. Mash 1 banana, spread it over the peanut butter, then sandwich with the other slice.

pancakes with bacon & maple syrup

Cost ££

Timing ●●

Serves 4

what you need

- 200 g (7 oz) self-raising flour
- 1 teaspoon baking powder
- pinch of cinnamon
- 1 egg, lightly beaten
- 150 ml (¼ pint) buttermilk
- 100 ml (3½ fl oz) milk
- 1 teaspoon vanilla extract
- 8 slices lean, smoked streaky bacon
- 15 g (½ oz) butter
- 2–4 tablespoons maple syrup, to serve

TIPS To boost hangover-beating antioxidants and potassium levels, serve these pancakes topped with slices of banana and summer berries instead of bacon.

what you do

1. Sift the flour, baking powder and cinnamon into a bowl and make a well in the centre. Pour in the eggs, buttermilk, milk and vanilla extract and beat to a smooth batter.
2. Place the bacon on a foil-lined baking sheet under a preheated grill for 5–6 minutes or until the fat has melted away and the bacon is crispy. Keep warm.
3. Melt a little butter in a large, nonstick frying pan over a medium heat and pour 4 spoonfuls of batter into the pan to make 4 small, thick pancakes. Cook for 2–3 minutes, then flip over and cook for a further 2–3 minutes until golden. Remove and repeat the process to make 12 pancakes, or until the batter is finished, stacking up the pancakes and keeping them warm.
4. Serve the pancakes in little piles with the crispy bacon and drizzled with the maple syrup.

croque monsieur

what you need

- 100 g (3½ oz) butter, softened
- 8 slices of white bread
- 4 slices of Cheddar cheese
- 4 slices of cooked ham
- 4 tablespoons vegetable oil
- pepper

what you do

1. Spread half the butter over one side of each slice of bread. Put a slice of Cheddar on 4 of the buttered slices, top with a slice of ham and sprinkle with pepper. Top with the remaining slices of bread, butter side down, and press down hard.

2. Melt half the rest of the butter with half the oil in a large frying pan, and fry 2 croques until golden brown, turning once. Cook the remaining 2 in the same way.

blueberry pancakes

what you need

Cost
££

Timing

Serves
4

- 250 ml (8 fl oz) milk
- 2 eggs
- 100 g (3½ oz) caster sugar
- 75 g (3 oz) butter, melted, plus extra for greasing
- 1 teaspoon baking powder
- pinch of salt
- 250 g (8 oz) plain flour
- 100 g (3½ oz) blueberries, plus extra to serve
- maple syrup or clear honey, to serve

what you do

1. Whisk together the milk, eggs, sugar and melted butter in a large bowl. Whisk in the baking powder and salt, add half the flour and whisk well until all the ingredients are incorporated, then whisk in the remaining flour. Stir in the blueberries to mix well.

2. Heat a large, nonstick pan over a medium-high heat. Grease the base of the pan with a little melted butter using kitchen paper. Lower the heat to medium. Spoon in large tablespoons of the batter until the pan is full, allowing a little space between each pancake. Add extra butter for frying if required.

3. Cook for 1–2 minutes on each side or until golden brown, then set aside and keep warm. Continue until all the batter is used.

4. Divide the pancakes between 4 plates and drizzle over a little maple syrup or honey. Serve immediately, with extra blueberries.

nachos with chipotle sauce

Cost ££

Timing ◑ ◑

Serves 4

what you need

- 200 g (7 oz) packet tortilla chips
- 200 g (7 oz) canned refried beans
- 200 g (7 oz) canned black beans, rinsed and drained
- 1 pickled jalapeño chilli, drained and sliced
- 150 g (5 oz) Cheddar cheese, grated

chipotle sauce

- 1 onion
- 3 tomatoes
- 2 garlic cloves, peeled and left whole
- 1 teaspoon chipotle paste
- salt and pepper

to serve

- 1 avocado, stoned, peeled and chopped
- handful of cherry tomatoes, halved
- handful of coriander leaves
- 4 tablespoons soured cream

what you do

Make the chipotle sauce. Heat a large, dry nonstick frying pan, add the onion and cook for 5 minutes, turning frequently. Add the tomatoes and cook for a further 5 minutes, then add the garlic and continue to cook for 3 minutes, or until the ingredients are softened and charred. Transfer to a food processor or blender and whizz to a coarse paste. Alternatively, mash well with a potato masher to make a chunky sauce. Leave to cool, then add the chipotle paste and season to taste. Set aside.

Place a layer of tortilla chips in a heatproof dish. Mix together the refried and black beans in a bowl, then spoon some of the beans over the chips and scatter with a layer of the chilli and cheese. Repeat the layers, finishing with a heavy layer of the cheese.

Bake in a preheated oven, 200°C (400°F), Gas Mark 6, for 7 minutes, or until the cheese has melted. Scatter over the avocado, tomato and coriander, drizzle with the chipotle sauce and soured cream and serve.

Index

Acknowledgements

Special photography: © Octopus Publishing Group/Stephen Conroy 6, 8, 9, 11, 28 (top left) 36, 48 (bottom right) 55, 56, 68 (bottom right) 90, 92 (bottom right), 94,97, 101, 110, 114 (bottom right),129, 131, 144 (top left and right), 146, 147, 148. 149, 150, 151, 152, 154, 155, 156 (top right), 158, 166; Vanessa Davies 114 (top left) 143; Will Heap 4 (bottom), 12 (bottom left) 22, 25, 27, 37, 51, 48 (top left), 59, 118, 121, 123, 126, 156 (bottom left), 170, 171; William Lingwood 45; David Munns 66, 103, 104, 105, 125, 136, 137, 142, 167; William Reavell 12 (top left), 16, 120, 160; Craig Robertson 4 (middle), 20, 84, 106; Lis Parsons 12 (bottom right), 15, 21, 28 (bottom left), 39, 46, 48 (top left), 63, 71, 72, 75, 76, 79, 80, 82, 89, 92 (bottom right), 111, 113, 114 (bottom left), 124, 133, 159, 168, 173; William Shaw 4 (top), 12 (top right), 19, 26, 28 (top right), 32, 41, 48 (bottom left), 52, 57, 60, 62, 68 (top and bottom left), 73, 78, 83, 86, 87, 92 (top left and right), 98, 114 (top right), 116, 130, 132, 135, 138, 141, 156 (top left and bottom right) 163, 165; Simon Smith 42; Ian Wallace 1, 28 (top right). 31, 35, 44, 64, 68 (top right), 91, 108, 144 (bottom right), 153, 163.

Additional photography: Shutterstock/123object 28 (cut-out top), 92 (cut-outs top and bottom), 114 (cut-out top right); EM Arts 156 (cut-out top); Evgeny Karandaev 144 (bottom left); Gemenacom 48 (cut-out bottom); gcpics 68 (cut-out bottom); johnfoto18 12 (cut-out bottom); Llashko 156 (cut-out bottom); Mariyana M 144 (cut-out top); mayakova 114 (cut-out top left); olavs 48 (cut-out top); Pinkyone 2-3, 10; spafra 244 (cut-out bottom); Valentina Razumova 68 (cut-out top); vnlit 28 (cut-out bottom); Volga 114 (cut-out bottom).